How to Start a Solo Law Practice

Hal Davis

How to Start a Solo Law Practice

Previous Edition Published as

Teach Me to Solo:
The Nuts and Bolts of Law Practice

by Hal Davis

Published by:
Hal Davis
PO Box 864379
Plano, TX 75086-4379 USA

Printed in the United States of America

Warning, Disclaimer

This book is designed to provide information on the business aspects of starting a solo law practice. It is sold with the understanding that the publisher and author are not engaged in rendering legal, accounting, or other professional services to those starting a law practice. If legal or other expert assistance is required, the services of a competent professional should be sought.

It is not the purpose of this manual to reprint all the information that is otherwise available to lawyers starting a law practice, but instead to complement, amplify and supplement other texts. You are urged to read all the available material, learn as much as possible about starting and running a law practice, and tailor the information to your individual needs.

Law practice is not a get-rich-quick scheme. Anyone who decides to start and run a law practice must expect to invest a lot of time and effort into it. For many people, running a solo law practice is more rewarding than working for a large firm or in a corporate or government legal section.

Every effort has been made to make this manual as complete and accurate as possible. However, there *may be mistakes,* both typographical and in content. Therefore, this text should be used only as a general guide and not as the ultimate source of starting and running a law practice. Furthermore, this book contains information on writing and publishing that is current only up to the printing date.

The purpose of this book is to educate and entertain. The author shall have neither liability nor responsibility to any person or entity with respect to any loss or damage caused, or alleged to have been caused, directly or indirectly, by the information contained in this book.

If you do not wish to be bound by the above, you may return this book to the publisher for a full refund.

Table of Contents

Acknowledgments

This book would not be possible without the help of so many people, and I must thank as many as I can. First, to Jana High of JLH Presentations, who first opened my eyes to the possibility of being an author, and who gave me the original title for this book. Dottie Walters, author of *Speak and Grow Rich*, was of inestimable help through her inspiring books, her pragmatic advice, and her ability to refer me to just the right person at just the right time. Chief among the people Dottie referred me to was Dan Poynter of Para Publishing who showed me with his books how I can become a published author, showed me the future of being an information provider, and also steered me to other folks whose help I needed. Dottie also referred me to Dan Kennedy, who has revolutionized the way I think about marketing my law practice.

I owe a huge debt to those who helped me start my law practice. Gerald Singer's book, *How to Go Directly Into the Solo Practice of Law Without Missing a Meal* was helpful and inspirational, but has been out of print for years. Jay Foonberg's *How to Start and Build a Law Practice* was chock-full of practical advice, is still being updated, and is more helpful now than before. My father, H. Sam Davis, Jr., a lawyer with a firm, is always there with encouragement and advice. My brother, Tom Davis, preceded me into forming his own firm and is always a telephone call away for sound advice.

Without the constant love and support of my wife, Ann, and my son, Read, I would not have had the vision to write this book.

Preface

I have an MBA degree in management, and my first career was a consultant to banks, primarily in data processing, cost accounting, and operational efficiency. I found myself as the Vice President of Operations and Data Processing for a five-bank holding company where I designed and managed the company's centralized operations center. Then, in 1987 the bottom fell out of the banking business in Texas and I lost my job. Nobody in banking was hiring, and prospective employers in other industries were afraid that when banking turned around I would leave for my native industry. I was unemployed and overqualified. I went back to school and got my law degree.

Having been laid off, I knew I wanted to be self-employed. I wanted to be sure I could never be laid off again. All through law school I planned to go into the solo practice of law, and I began asking questions of my law professors. I asked if we could bring in a speaker to talk about how to set up your own law office: everything from choosing office space to picking office management software. My professors were just not interested in doing this, and I didn't have the time or contacts to do it myself.

I found two books in the law library that helped me tremendously: Jay Foonberg's *How to Start and Build a Law Practice*, and Gerald Singer's *How to Go Directly Into the Solo Practice of Law Without Missing a Meal.* I found later editions of each and I read them cover to cover. Mr. Foonberg's book has been updated and is available from the American Bar Association's bookstore.

As good as the advice was in those two books, I did not have a technologically savvy solo lawyer available to help me with the business decisions I faced in setting up my new firm. But I had a number of advantages that most new lawyers don't have, and I was able to figure things out without too much trouble. But I would have loved to have someone help me with the problems I faced.

In my ninth year of practicing law I realized I had become the person that I wanted to talk to 11 years ago. There had to be people graduating from law school now with a desire to be self-employed but with no real plan for locating their office, finding software and hardware, or finding business. These are the people I wanted to help with my seminars and my book.

For the book to be as useful as possible to the reader, I knew I had to make very specific recommendations on computer hardware and software. But I also knew that this would make the book out of date very quickly. Fortunately, advances in publishing technology have made it feasible to update a book much more frequently. It is my goal to revise this book frequently.

I wish you the best of luck in building your law practice, and I hope this book helps. Please send me your success stories or suggestions for improving this book to hdavis@planolaw.com.

Preface to the Second Edition

Don't be confused. This is the first edition of How to Start a Solo Law Practice. But it's the second edition of my book. The first edition was published under the title, *Teach Me to Solo: The Nuts and Bolts of Law Practice.* I found that title to be too cute and insufficiently informative, and coupled with my whimsical cover design, I had a hard time getting the book into stores.

As is so often true in life, where I thought I was going after the first edition of this book is different from where I have gone. I had plans to be a professional speaker and trainer for new lawyers, and I have wandered away from that vision. However, in trying to learn how to market this book and my speaking career, I have learned a great deal about marketing, and have applied it to my law practice with good results. Incorporating what I have learned about marketing is the primary impetus for this second edition.

Along the way, I also became aware that much of what was in the first edition was fluff. For example, I spent many long hours learning about typography and typeface selection, and I tried to pass that on to my readers, but with perspective I know that if my readers find it as interesting as I have, they will find the information elsewhere. Few who will buy this book from its title will care which typeface they use in their correspondence.

I believe you will find the second edition a much tighter, more meaningful guide to starting a solo law practice. Or at least I hope so.

Chapter 1
You Can Do It

This book is about living the American Dream. About living the dream of the founding fathers. About going into business for yourself, all by yourself. The pure dream of independence and dedication.

This book is about freedom. The freedom to work as many hours as you believe necessary. The freedom to balance business and personal life as you see fit. The freedom to choose your areas of practice, and to take whatever causes you believe are just.

This book is about gratification. About having a personal relationship with every client, instead of having directions filtered down from a senior partner. About choosing a direction you know is right without being second-guessed by someone with only a tangential connection with the case.

This book is about making money. Billing four hours a day all by yourself is more profitable than billing eight hours a day for someone else.

This book is about risk. Not taking more risk, or less risk, just a different kind of risk. Working for a big firm may seem less risky (if that's an opportunity that's available), but thousands of attorneys are laid off from big firms every year, and suddenly the paycheck from the big firm isn't secure at all.

As Jay Foonberg put it, this book is for the 19 out of 20 law students that don't graduate in the top 5% of their class, and don't have a job waiting for them in a large law firm. This book is also for those who did graduate in the top five percent but have the vision, the independence, and the grit to do it their own way right from the start. This book is for lawyers who have been toiling in someone else's vineyard for years and are now ready to harvest the satisfaction of working for yourself.

Each year each big law firm hires dozens of recent graduates. Over the next decade those new hires will work very hard for somebody else, having their every decision second-guessed, and seldom having direct contact with the client. Many will live in fear that the brief they prepared wasn't exactly what the partner wanted and they'll have to do it again. Yet despite their anguish and diligence, only a small percent will be elevated to partner with that firm within a decade. The others will leave the firm to join with other lawyers in a new firm, or will leave the practice of law entirely. Or they will open their own solo practice.

What's wrong with these people? Why didn't they make partner? After all, they were in the top of their class, or they wouldn't have gotten the job in the first place. Well, legal education isn't everything. For one thing, each new lawyer in a big firm works for a partner. Partners may be very poor managers. A law degree does not prepare one for management any more than it prepares one for the solo practice of law. Talk to an unhappy young lawyer in a large firm, and you'll find someone who can't figure out what his boss wants.

When I was in law school, I was determined to go directly into solo law practice. I had been a management consultant and a vice president in a bank holding company, and I had learned that the only true job security was working for yourself. But when I discussed this with my fellow students, the response was often, "I plan to go solo eventually, but I want to practice in a big firm for a while, first."

Working for a firm before going solo is only a good idea if you don't know that you want to be a solo when you leave law school. Solo lawyers will start off making less money than their friends who go to work for a large firm. The big firm pay will be addictive, and the golden handcuffs will keep you from breaking free voluntarily. You won't be able to make the break until someone decides you're not partner material and you are laid off. Or the firm dissolves. Either way, you're looking at a large cut in pay and having to go solo on short notice.

Large law firms are an historical anomaly. Until a couple of generations ago, a large law firm was a half-dozen lawyers. Those who would be lawyers "clerked" for a lawyer, often doing the same work that a photocopier does today. Ironically, as the twentieth century brought us so many tools that made it so much easier to practice law alone, we also saw the dominance of huge law firms.

What makes the big firms work is specialization and carefully chosen areas of practice. At the bottom are the new lawyers who are expected to bill well over 2000 hours each year. In the middle are those who still bill plenty of hours, but are more focused on supervising and training young lawyers than on directly doing billable work. At the top are the rainmakers that develop, cultivate, and maintain relationships with clients. And, of course, the source of all of this activity is the client, chosen by the firm because of their ability to spin off thousands of hours of work year after year.

But this book is also for those who find themselves working for somebody else in the practice of law and now want to work for themselves.

The economics of solo practice

In 2003, large firms were paying their new hires from the top of the class of the top law schools about $100,000 per year, were billing them out at fees of at least $150 per hour, and were expecting their hires to bill 2000 hours per year. Out of $300,000 in annual billings from the new hire, the firm paid $100,000 in salary, $20,000 in benefits, and perhaps $30,000 to apply to rent, the law library, and support staff. The other $150,000 repaid the firm for finding the client, recruiting and training the new hire, and having the capitalistic gumption to pull it all together.

But that's not all the firm gets out of it. Not a single written word from the new hire goes to the client without review from managers, partners, and senior partners, each with a higher billing rate. And, of course, not a single word from the client goes to the new hire without being filtered through the same people. Every week the senior partner, the partner, the manager, and the new hire will have a meeting to discuss the status of the case, at a combined hourly billing rate exceeding $1,000. Hiring a big firm costs a lot of money.

It may be that big firms are the only ones able to handle some of the biggest, most complex types of cases. But there are much more efficient ways to practice law, and equally rewarding opportunities for the new lawyer.

A lawyer going directly into solo practice in 2003 could also bill himself at $150 per hour. The rent would be less than $1,000 per month, and all other monthly expenses should be less than another $1,000 per month, for a monthly "nut" of $2,000. Because the lawyer is self-employed and pays both the employer and employee payroll taxes, the self-employed lawyer here needs to bill (and collect) $150,000 per year to have an effective salary of $100,000. In this case, that comes to 1,000 hours per year, or about four hours per day, or half the load of the lawyer in the big firm. Of course, because of the absence of support personnel, the self-employed lawyer will spend a significant amount of time every day performing non-billable tasks, such as rounding up new business and paying the bills. The first-year self-employed lawyer probably will not have 1,000 hours of billable work to do in the first year, and will probably not make $100,000. But our lawyer will spend a great deal of the first year making valuable contacts in the local bar associations, chamber of commerce, volunteer organizations, and generally becoming involved in the community.

As the practice grows, many lawyers will hire support staff. That is a decision each lawyer needs to make. I used to counsel against it. I now do the math this way. As soon as the lawyer has more to do in a day than can be done alone, it's time to hire staff. If a solo lawyer is to make an effective salary of $100,000 per year and cover overhead, working about 2000 hours per year (billable and unbillable), then the value of the lawyer's time is somewhere in the vicinity of $100 per hour. If there's a task that can be done for a $20 per hour employee, and that frees up time for the solo lawyer to work on the strategy and tactics of growing and controlling the business, then it's silly to have the lawyer do these tasks.

Having said that, it is a grave error for the brand-new self-employed lawyer to start off with staff. First of all, paying a living wage to a legal assistant means that the lawyer must earn two living wages if one is to be brought home.

More importantly, no manager can effectively hire, train, and supervise someone if the manager doesn't thoroughly understand the job. The lawyer can't properly supervise an employee until the lawyer has done the employee's job.

Mark is a lawyer who went into solo practice upon leaving a medium-sized law firm at the invitation of the firm. He hired a seasoned legal assistant with whom he had worked in the past, even though he did not know where the assistant's paycheck was going to come from. Several months later, the assistant had to take several weeks of medical leave, Mark was in the middle of a trial, and he hired a secretary from a temporary agency. The secretary was sufficiently trained, *but not on Mark's way of doing business.* The secretary didn't know how to answer the phone, where to file correspondence, or even the office style for formatting letters.

The best way to hire staff is to have done all of the work yourself, then decide what parts of the job would be best done by someone else. Document the procedures, train someone from the documentation, and then review the documentation to see if it accurately reflects the procedures. Build an office stylebook, a procedure handbook, and a script for some of the basic tasks, such as answering the phone and making appointments. Then, when the secretary quits or is sick, you can get the work done without an assistant, and can get a new hire up to speed quickly from the documentation.

Chapter 2
Areas of Practice

The first decision for the new lawyer is to choose the type of law to practice. If the lawyer is leaving a large firm he or she already has a proven area of expertise to capitalize on, and may even be able to steal a few clients from the firm to get things started.

The temptation is to hold oneself out as a general practitioner, able to handle whatever needs a client may have. After all, the lawyer is licensed to practice in any area of the law, except a few very specialized areas, such as patents. But people do not hire lawyers because they can solve a variety of problems, but because the lawyer can solve the particular problem the client is facing now.

Imagine you have a clogged drain in your home, and you are looking in the yellow pages for someone to fix it. It's unlikely you'd be attracted to someone who advertises as a general plumber. You'd probably pick out someone who claims to be a drain-clearing specialist. By the same token when clients look for lawyers, they want someone as narrowly focused on their specific problem as possible.

I recommend that you develop two or three areas of expertise, and that you market them independently. I normally carry two completely different sets of business cards, so I'll have the right card for the prospect. I have a version of my letterhead for each line of business. I even have a different web site (not just a web page) for each line of business. It's tempting to recommend that you focus exclusively on one area, but our society changes too quickly for that and many lawyers have had their entire practice evaporate when the law changed. For example, in Texas many lawyers earned a very good living representing injured workers. Then, in 1991 the legislature amended the law and Worker's Comp virtually disappeared as a source of income for lawyers. Those who had another area of practice to develop were not hit as hard as those who had only one type of business.

Services to individuals are comparatively easy to get by way of advertising, word of mouth, and standing in the community. These services include divorce, criminal defense, personal bankruptcy, and wills and estate planning. The problem with services to individuals is that as your expertise grows and your billing rate rises, fewer and fewer individuals will be able to afford your work. Also, there is little opportunity for follow-on work. Individuals tend to need a lawyer only a few times in their lifetimes. Lawyers find that they are continually having to find new clients and realize very little value from continued relationships.

Services to organizations are nearly opposite. It may take a very long time to sign up that first utility company to draw up a right-of-way agreement with the city. But once you do, that utility company will need more agreements with other cities, and you can establish a relationship with other utility companies and other cities. You will develop a long-term relationship with a client, and reasonable escalations in your billing rate are expected and meet with little resistance. Both litigation and transactional work can be done for organizations.

I recommend that the new solo lawyer develop one area of practice with services to individuals, and another area of practice with services to organizations.

Bill learned the lesson of marketing each practice area to its own target market. Bill practiced divorce and evictions. He volunteered at a local divorce support group, and when people asked what he did, he'd say that he was a lawyer that practiced divorce and evictions. This merely confused the people he was talking with, and he got very few referrals. But Bill learned to wear different hats. In the divorce support group he was a divorce lawyer. When he visited the apartment owners' associations, he was an eviction lawyer, and did not mention divorces.

The more narrowly you can cast yourself, the more narrowly you will describe your target client, and the easier it will be to reach your target. This point cannot be overemphasized. Good advertising *excludes* prospects that do not fit the desired profile. By saying who your client is *not*, you make the true prospect feel that this is really for him or her.

Suppose I were selling golf equipment. This would narrow my universe of prospective customers to several million. If I had products that focused on female golfers, I'd cut the size of my prospect list by more than half (more men play golf than women). If I limited it to left-handed female golfers, I'd cut the universe down by another 80%. Now while I'd have fewer people who could buy my services, consider the advantages. I'd really know the specific problems of my customers. I'd know what they liked, didn't like, what publications they read, and much more. More important, it's far more likely that left-handed female golfers would tell other left-handed female golfers that Hal Davis is *the* supplier. There'd be a natural network, and I could certainly craft a focused newsletter. Any advertising I did could start off with "Hey, southpaw lady golfers! Are you tired of golf equipment made for someone else?" When my prospects read the ad, they'd say to themselves, "He's talking to *me!*"

The more narrowly you define your field of expertise, the more quickly and easily you can establish yourself as a leading authority in that field. I know 3 (and only 3) lawyers in Texas that only prepare documents to divide retirement benefits in divorces, as subcontractors for the divorce lawyers in the case. I know of an attorney who is the leading authority on intellectual property law for authors who have become publishers of their own works. I know of an attorney who is a leading authority on helping real estate investors use land trusts to contain liability on rental properties. Each of these lawyers has a very clear idea who his or her clients are, and knows what magazines to write articles for, what conventions to give speeches at, and where to find lists to send direct mail to.

This is your "Unique Selling Proposition" or USP. It does not have to be a particularly narrow area of legal practice. But you do have to give someone a reason a unique reason to choose you over all the other available options. You could be the lawyer without a waiting room. The lawyer where you get a chair massage while you get legal advice. The lawyer who practices in his own coffee shop (or bowling alley). The lawyer to the Korean community. The personal injury lawyer for hawg riders.

Take the time right now to jot down some ideas on areas of practice where you have industry experience, or that particularly interested you in law school, or where you have connections to draw upon in finding clients. Try to segment and define your target market by age, gender, profession, industry, location, income, ethnic origin, etc.

Chapter 3
Advertising

Any law practice that needs to add clients should do some advertising. The bigger the need to add clients, the bigger the need to advertise. The more the practice is geared to services for individuals, the greater the need to advertise. But advertising must also be highly targeted to be cost-effective.

Advertising is only a portion of marketing. Marketing involves picking a market to sell to, designing a product, and making the market aware of the product. Before an advertising plan can be drawn up, the product and market need to be clearly identified. The advertising plan for $399 uncontested divorces should be vastly different from the advertising plan for a $10,000 comprehensive review of personnel policies and procedures in the fiberglass boat manufacturing industry.

Once the market is clearly identified, all it takes is reasoning, investigation, and hard work to develop an advertising plan to sell to that market.

Sometimes when I have a cold and am too sick to go to work, I'll turn on the television during the day at home. I will be bombarded with ads from personal injury lawyers. But that really only makes sense. Maybe only a small percentage of the viewers will be injured people thinking of hiring a lawyer. But on the other hand, a comparatively high percentage of injured people thinking of hiring a lawyer will be home watching television. This may be a comparatively cost-effective way of reaching this audience.

Right or wrong, many states have drawn up lawyer ethics codes that prohibit a lawyer from making direct contact with an individual who may need legal services. It is viewed as purer and somehow nobler when the individual begins an investigation of lawyers available without pressure from an individual lawyer. Personal injury lawyers point out that lawyers often make direct contact with corporations for their legal work without any problems at all. The justice of this system can be debated in another time and place. The lesson is that the individual lawyer must be very careful to do only what is legal and ethical in his or her own state. Sending a bouquet of flowers and a get-well card to an accident victim you've never met can lose you your license.

Many states also place restrictions on attorney advertising. Be sure to check with your state bar association before buying any advertising.

Image Advertising

Most advertising is "image advertising." The ad creates an image of the advertiser, with the hope that when a need develops for the advertiser's product, the advertiser will be "top of mind" and will be the supplier selected. Perhaps the ultimate example of this is Coca-Cola. The company spends untold millions (billions?) of dollars each year putting its image or message *everywhere,* from the sides of buses, to billboards, to the fronts of soft drink dispensing machines in restaurants, to television ads, to blimps. It's impossible to think of purchasing a soft drink without being aware that one option is Coca-Cola.

One problem with image advertising is that it costs a *lot* of money to develop an image.

A second problem with image advertising is that it's nearly impossible to determine which ads were most effective in creating the desired image, so the advertiser never has a clear idea which parts of the advertising budget were well spent. Can you imagine ordering a Coke and have the waiter ask you, "where did you see our ad?" or "how did you hear about Coke?" Of course, with a really huge budget some educated guesses can be made. For instance, Coke could implement advertising on the sides of buses in Cleveland but not in Dayton, and see if they can detect any difference in sales.

Image advertising has two goals. The first is to associate the name of the product or service with a positive visceral response, often expressed with a single word. An example might be a full-page ad in the newspaper, with the logo of a bank in the middle, and above it is the single word, "Security." Lots of white space.

The second goal is to pervade either the marketplace, or at least the point of sale, with the image so that when the buying decision is made, the image, the product or service, and the visceral reaction all come together to influence the purchase decision.

Imagine the implications for the solo lawyer marketing legal services. Even aside from the expense of developing an image and designing an advertising strategy, the cost to pervade the marketplace is simply prohibitive.

Image advertising can be adapted to the small business, although it can be questioned whether the result is "true" image advertising. I am intrigued by the work of Peter Montoya and Tim Vandehey in their book and seminar titled, *The Brand Called You* (book © 1999 Millenium Advertising, Costa Mesa, CA, ISBN 0-9674506-0-8, www.milladv.com). They are most closely targeted to financial planners, but it's directly applicable to lawyers as well (and, I suppose, plastic surgeons, orthodontists, and all sorts of other professionals).

Montoya and Vandehey walk you through developing an advertising image, and then encourage you to get the image to your prospects through direct mail, such as with monthly post cards or newsletters.

One real problem with most kinds of advertising for many lawyers is that it is very difficult to target your prospects so you can market to them. A lawyer who works in securing or litigating liens on real estate may be able to reach his target quite efficiently through the conventions attended and publications read by general contractors. A personal injury lawyer may be able to reach persons unable to work by advertising on daytime television. But a divorce lawyer may be frustrated because he can't find a magazine called "Thinking About Getting Divorced" that he can advertise in or buy the mailing list.

Direct Response Advertising

While image ads will have lots of "white space" and will be heavy on concept, direct response ads will have lots and lots of words. Each direct response ad contains a "call to action" and the effectiveness of the ad can be judged by how many viewers of the ad took the action requested. Direct response print ads will have coupons; radio and TV ads will have toll-free phone numbers; and web sites will have a "<u>click here to order</u>." There will often be an extension number after the phone number, or a department number, or a person to ask for, and this is almost always to track which ad prompted the response, so that the advertising message and media can be continually tweaked.

One-Step and Two-Step Marketing

Most folks like to advertise "single step" marketing, like a yellow pages ad for a carpet cleaner that asks the reader to call for an appointment. This works well when the advertising medium is well-targeted to your prospects.

But many advertisers have found it more cost-effective to use multi-step advertising. I've heard it said that image advertising is to "get your name out there," but that direct response advertising is designed to "get their names in here;" that developing a list of folks interested in your product is more important that getting the image of the advertiser into the marketplace.

One trick to doing effective direct mail campaigns is developing a list of people who are likely "suspects" (as opposed to qualified prospects) for your services. Perhaps you represent folks in traffic court. It may be fairly easy to obtain a list of folks who have gotten traffic tickets and send a letter to each of them. If you write wills, maybe you'd rent a list of subscribers to magazines targeted to retirees. These are examples of one-step marketing.

But, often there is no list of folks in your area. There is no "Thinking About a Divorce" magazine whose list you can rent. In this case, you may choose to do "two-step" advertising, where the object of the first step is to generate a list of suspects that you can market to. For example, I might run a classified ad that says, "Divorce can be simple and easy. Free Report: 1-800-xxx-xxxx." People could call in, leave their addresses, and I'd mail them a free report. And then I'd have a list of people who were interested in divorce, and I could start sending them a newsletter or letter campaign. Instead of renting a list from a list broker, I'd have made my own list for the price of the ad and the cost of creating a report and mailing it.

The key here is to create an irresistible offer. You have to get the attention of people who are interested in your product, and then offer something they just can't pass up. This is often an "information product" such as a report, publication, guide, or something similar, and it's usually free.

Lawyers often advertise a free consultation, but I don't believe that's a very good offer, for several reasons. Mostly, there's too much commitment required from the prospect, and it requires too much sustained effort on the part of the prospect to satisfy the need. If the prospect just picks up the phone (at 3 a.m. on Saturday), hears a recorded announcement, and leaves his mailing address, he has "scratched his itch" with a very small investment of time, money, and planning. But if the prospect were responding to a free consultation offer, he'd have to make a note to himself to call you on Monday, then actually call you, perhaps play phone tag, schedule the appointment, then drive to the appointment, invest a half hour in your office, and perhaps be subjected to a long sales pitch.

Now maybe the prospect has to have the big itch and has to go to all of the hassle to come to see you in order to become a client. But the purpose of the lead generation ad is to find those who have the little itch, so that you can stay in contact with them until it becomes a big itch.

The lead generation ad could direct someone to a web site, or an email autoresponder, but I don't do that very much. First, if my ad is being delivered via a newspaper or magazine ad, or by radio advertising, it's highly likely that a telephone will be available to immediately scratch the itch, but if the prospect must find a computer, it's likely that the itch will be forgotten by the time for response arrives. Equally important, the entire point of the exercise was for me to get contact information for the prospect. And as difficult as it is to get folks to open a letter, it's exponentially more difficult to get folks to see your email as a pearl amongst the spam.

There's an advertising adage that has a number of variants, but the one I prefer is this: "Marketing is the process of delivering the right message, to the right prospect, at the right time." Direct response advertising is all about the first two: the right message and the right prospect. But it's exceedingly difficult to project the right time. One response to this is to advertise in the yellow pages, on the theory that the prospect won't be in the yellow pages until the time is right. But the yellow pages is also full of the messages of your competitors.

Follow-Up

My mentor for marketing and advertising has been Dan Kennedy. He has developed his *Magnetic Marketing Toolkit,* (www.DanKennedy.com) which is a structured series of three letters to prospects. Once you've found a prospect, it's comparatively inexpensive to continue to market to the prospect until the prospect turns into a client. This is an attempt to control the third part of the advertising adage, by reaching the prospect *at the right time.*

Of course, there's no real magic to three letters. Once you've identified someone with that little itch, there's very little limit to how many times, or how many ways, you can stay in touch with them. Letters, newsletters, email, fax broadcast, voice broadcast, personal phone calls, trinkets sent in the mail, and other approaches are great ways to make sure that when that little itch turns into a big itch, there's something to remind the prospect that you're the best back scratcher around.

Marketing Math

Dan Kennedy has an axiom that goes something like, "Direct response marketing is equal parts behavioral psychology and math." The behavioral psychology part is learning to write good advertising copy, as Dan teaches in his seminars and published materials. The math part is the simple arithmetic of keeping track of how much money you spent on a marketing activity and comparing it to the results you got. And it's the math that will tell you how many letters you can afford to send to a prospect.

Suppose you're a divorce lawyer, and you charge $1,000 for a divorce. You run an ad in a local magazine or newspaper for $500 offering a free report. You get 10 requests, and spend $30 for the answering service to take the calls, and $20 in photocopying and postage to get the reports out to the prospects. Your lead generation advertising cost was $500 for 10 leads, or $50 per lead. Then you had "chasing costs" or "fulfillment costs) of another $5 per lead.

Now let's assume you did this 10 times with similar results, so you've got 100 prospects in your database. You write a letter, have it copied, stuffed, and mailed to your 100 prospects, for a total cost of $200 including labor, copying, and postage. Four of your prospects turn into clients, with a profit of $400 each, or $1,600 total. You spent $200 and earned $1,600, so clearly this was a profitable mailing.

Next month you send out another mailing, and maybe you only get two or three responses. But it doesn't take much mathematical ability to see that as long as you're spending less than $400 to get a new client, it's worthwhile. So you do the math on every mailing, and decide when you've reached the point of diminishing returns. Most lawyers can afford to stay in touch for a very long time without the costs of staying in touch exceeding the value of the prospect becoming a client.

Lifetime Value of a Customer

But there's more to the math than deciding whether it's cost effective to send another letter or newsletter. We still haven't decided whether it was cost-effective to spend $55 per lead to generate our list of prospects.

Many of the products sold on infomercials on television are sold at a loss. That is, the margin on each sale may be insufficient to pay for the cost of running the ad. Many marketers will cheerfully acquire clients while losing money on each one because they know they can make plenty of money from subsequent sales to the same customer. A perfect example of this is skin cream. If the glop is half as good as the advertising says it is, customers are going to want more after the first batch runs out. Some customers will even ask that their credit card be charged $9.95 every month so that a new shipment of glop will be sent out once a quarter.

A tax lawyer who earns $300 in fees preparing a simple income tax return may be willing to spend more than $300 in advertising to get a new client because he knows the client will come back year after year. If the average client stays for 5.5 years, then the lifetime value of a client in this case is 5.5 times $300 or $1,650 (on a revenue basis, not a profit basis). Knowing this, the tax lawyer may figure it's worth spending considerably more than $300 to get a new client.

On the other hand, as a divorce lawyer may not be able to think of any legal services that are readily marketable to former divorce clients. In this case, the lifetime value of a client is simply the average value of a single divorce engagement.

Let's get back to our example of spending $500 on a newspaper or magazine ad. Your analysis is that the lifetime value of a divorce client is $1,000. Now, that's revenue, not profit, and there are costs associated with running your office, so clearly you're not willing to spend $1,000 to get a client worth $1,000, because then you're working for free, and not even contributing to rent and office expenses. So, it's good to know what you want to consider your cost to produce a product, to know when you're selling it a loss or at a profit.

Referrals from Clients

Of course, the whole equation changes if you're able to find a way to get your current and past clients to regularly refer new clients to you. If the lifetime value of a client is $1,000 excluding referrals, and if you could consistently get each client to refer another client to you, then you've greatly increased the lifetime value of the client.

Continuity

The holy grail of direct marketers is continuity. If one is selling a newsletter, then you have an agreement to send them a newsletter every month and charge their credit card every month until they take action to tell you to stop. The legal equivalent of this is prepaid legal services, where you get the premium every month. This greatly increases the revenue achieved after the client has been found. I haven't found a way for me to make this work in my practice, but if you're able to find a way in your practice, you'll find that it can be cost effective for you to spend astronomical sums to acquire a new client.

Yellow Pages

Lawyers love yellow pages advertising. And the yellow pages love lawyers. The reasoning is sound: where do people go when they want to find a lawyer? But I do not believe that yellow pages advertising is cost-effective for most attorneys because it is too crowded and too expensive.

"Attorneys" is typically the second-thickest listing in any yellow pages. In each book there is page after page of full-page ads costing thousands of dollars each month. Even if I could afford a full-page ad, the odds are dismal that I'd be able to attract more than a small percentage of those browsing the yellow pages looking for a lawyer. The odds are made even worse by the fragmentation of the yellow pages market: there are so many yellow pages publications serving my market that I'd have to advertise in them all to get adequate coverage. My office is in Plano, which is a suburb of Dallas. I've had the following yellow pages delivered to my office: The Southwestern Bell Greater Dallas Yellow Pages, The Southwestern Bell Richardson/Garland/Plano Yellow Pages, the GTE Richardson/Plano Book, The Silver Pages (a directory aimed at seniors), The Plano Book from Gordon Publications, The Shepherd's Guide for Greater Dallas, The

Shepherd's Guide for Collin and Denton Counties, and several others.

I have not found yellow pages advertising to be cost-effective, but I do not practice personal injury law. If you believe that yellow pages advertising may be cost-effective for you, there is a way to test market it. You can obtain an additional telephone number that will appear only in your yellow pages ad. It will still ring only to your regular incoming line, but the telephone company will count the calls made to that phone number and provide you with statistics periodically. Ask your yellow pages salesman.

The salesman will pursue a line of logic that will convince you that only one or two additional cases per month will pay for the ad. While that may be true, you did not enter the practice of law to work to pay for an ad. You want to bring money home for your work. Consider that telephone solicitors make random calls to every telephone number, so the call counts from the telephone company are going to include calls to the special yellow pages ad tracking number. Also, prospective clients that heard of you from other sources may look in the yellow pages to find you and will call on the ad tracking telephone number. Finally, consider that you have just spent considerable money promoting a telephone number other than your regular one, so there is considerable pressure to keep that telephone number for several years.

One fundamental tenet of direct response (measurable) advertising is to test, test, test. You run an ad and measure the results. Then change a little something and measure the results. If the change got a higher result, then keep it.

Otherwise, scrap it and change something else. This does not work well in yellow pages advertising, where one usually cannot change an ad for at least a year (and the bills keep coming in whether the ad works or not).

Newsletters

A fruitful area for advertising is in the newsletters of the organizations to which you belong. Here, the advertisement does not try to introduce you to people, but to remind people you know about what you do and how to get in touch with you. Your church, your child's school, your political party, your public service organizations, your art groups, and your hobby groups will usually have newsletters, and will typically insert an ad which is simply a reproduction of your business card for a few dollars a year.

Some organizations have a newcomer's guide to the community, with information such as frequency of trash pickup, how to contact the water utilities, and so on. Often these guides will accept advertising for local merchants, and many attorneys have found this a productive place to advertise.

Internet

The Internet is growing as an advertising medium for lawyers. If you put up a web page that contains the word lawyer, you will receive several email solicitations to join some sort of online attorney finder. These can be a good source of referrals, especially if you have a web site that provides the consumer with useful information.

It is difficult to track the effectiveness of a particular Internet ad unless the service provides you with click-through information. If you ask your caller how they got your name, they will often say, "I found you on the Internet," which does not do any good in determining which lawyer referral sites are good investments. Also check with your web site host to see if they have statistical tracking information to tell you where people are coming from when they hit your site.

I have found advertising on the Internet to be frustrating. It offers by far the highest return on my investment, but I find it difficult to figure out how to throw more money at it to get better results.

I'm probably going to date this book very quickly here, but the hard part is getting your page to show up well in the search engines. The trick is to figure out which phrases people are going to use when they are looking for someone like you. Then you find and hire an expert who will try to make your key phrases point to you at the top of the search engines. This is much harder than it sounds, but it is definitely worth the effort.

If your print or broadcast advertising drives people to a web site, you have compounded your problems in tracking the effectiveness of your ads. There is no simple, effective way of tracking which print ad or radio ad produced the hit on the web site. If you ask the client, they'll just say the found you on the web, or using a search engine, because it's much "hipper" to have found you on the web than from an ad in the shopper newspaper. You can create a bunch of lead-in sub-sites, such as "www.planolaw.com/greensheet" or "www.planolaw.com/kluv", but most folks will just type the part before the slash. The only real way to track is to get a bunch of domains registered, such as "haldavisdivorcelawyer.com", "haldavisdivorcelaw.com" and "haldavisfamilylaw.com" and use a different one in each ad.

Focus on the audience

The most important advice on advertising is to determine your market before you choose the advertising to reach it. If you plan to do divorces, it is not enough to find people who want a divorce: you also need people who can afford to pay your fees. Advertising in a medium that reaches primarily lower-income people may only be cost-effective if you have an extremely streamlined minimum fee system in place, with high volume and several clerks or secretaries.

If your market is building contractors, you'll want to find out what organizations they belong to, what newsletters and magazines they read, and what conferences they attend. You'll want to write an article or develop a program that is of benefit to contractors and establish yourself as an expert servicing their industry.

As a general rule you will not find it cost-effective to advertise in media that are not well targeted to your specific market. Radio and television may offer fairly high numbers of viewers/listeners per dollar, but only a very small portion will be in your targeted industry or geographical area.

Chapter 4
Other Sources
of New Clients

Advertising is often the first idea for any new lawyer starting a practice, but there are much more cost-effective ways of getting new clients that should be explored as well.

Referral services

Most cities and states have lawyer referral services. The service will buy a large ad in the yellow pages to solicit calls from people seeking to hire a lawyer. The service may have several lists, such as divorce, traffic tickets, consumer protection, general criminal, landlord/tenant, civil, and bankruptcy. Most of the callers to this service will be individuals rather than businesses, so it is most effective for building a retail practice.

The referral service will usually charge a fee to cover the costs of advertising and for the clerical staff to answer the phone 24 hours per day. Fees may be a flat fee per year for as many practice area lists as the lawyer cares to join, or there may be an annual fee for each list. Some may require a forwarding fee based on a percentage of legal fees collected on a referred case.

Referral services usually require that all attorneys provide proof of professional malpractice insurance, which is a barrier that keeps many attorneys from listing with referral services. Depending on your area of practice, expect to spend a thousand dollars or so for your first year's coverage with a $100,000 policy and a $5,000 deductible. See the chapter on insurance for the lawyer near the back of this book.

There have been a number of abuses with referral services. Sometimes one attorney would buy a big ad for a referral service, and the only attorney every referred by the service was the one attorney. Or several attorneys would form a referral service, with only one attorney in each practice area. When the public finds out about such arrangements, they feel cheated and view lawyers negatively.

Several states have requirements that referral services must pass before a lawyer may legally or ethically list with them. For example, a service serving a particular geographical area must accept all attorneys who pass certain criteria, such as license in good standing, office location in the geographical area, malpractice insurance, and so on.

Some referral services require that the fee for the initial consultation is paid to the referral service, and others require that the initial consultation be free or of minimal cost to the consumer. Check with your state bar association on any legal or ethical requirements on referral services.

Networking groups

Many attorneys have found success in networking groups. These are clubs that meet weekly or monthly, usually for breakfast or lunch, for the purpose of referring business to each other. Membership will often be limited to one person in each industry or area, although there may be several attorneys if their areas of practice do not conflict.

Here's a common agenda for a networking group. First, the membership will engage in informal conversation before the group begins its formal meeting. The meeting will be called to order and each person will be encouraged to give a one-minute commercial about who they are, what they do, and what types of persons would be a good referral prospect for them. At the end of the one-minute commercials, one member of the group will have a turn for a longer, more detailed presentation, of perhaps ten minutes duration. The group may then exchange leads and thanks for leads that come to fruition during the last week or month.

Networking groups can be an excellent way to break into legal work for businesses. Take care to define yourself narrowly enough that your commercial will jar others into thinking of organizations in that category. Lawyers advertising simply "business law" will usually attract less business than those giving a more specific area of practice, such as employer/employee relations in the funeral home industry will.

Membership in most networking groups is by invitation only, so you'll have to be invited in or form your own. The best way to be invited is to be in another networking group, so the trick is to find a group that will allow people to join without an invitation. Frequently the easiest path to a networking group is through the local chamber of commerce.

One of the most important skills is the one-minute commercial. It needs to be catchy and clear about the area of practice solicited. A benefit often overlooked about networking is that it teaches skills that are useful in other settings, such as a neighborhood association meeting or a cocktail party. A lawyer should be always ready to quickly and clearly state the precise business he or she is in.

Networking is a learned art form and every new attorney should learn it. There are many unwritten codes of networking that will make the novice networker unwelcome.

One of the best networkers I know is Jana High. She'd always start her one-minute commercial with, "Hi! [pause] I'm Jana High!" so it became hard to say, "Hi!" to someone without thinking of Jana.

You may also want to build a moniker for yourself. Every networking group will have a pool guy, a banker lady, an insurance dude, and so on. Decide what you want to be called and start calling introducing yourself that way. If there's something distinctive about you (*e.g.*, you always wear a cowboy hat), carry that forward to everything you do, such as putting a picture of a cowboy hat on your business cards, your letterhead, and all your advertising.

Take the time right now to jot down some thoughts on your one-minute commercial using one of the blank pages near the back of this book. Use only one area of practice, and be fairly specific about your target market. Use your name at the first and last of the commercial and try working in some sort of play on your name.

Referrals

Always ask for referrals, from your clients, from other attorneys, from family members, and from members of civic organizations. Lawyers like to look prosperous, and people like to refer business to prosperous people, but it is easy to appear so prosperous that you do not need additional business. Counteract the too-busy image by asking for referrals.

Always let your referring source know that you appreciate the referral. Expressions of appreciation do not have to be expensive to be effective. Handwritten thank-you notes are a must. I will sometimes enclose a five-dollar gift certificate to a local ice cream parlor.

The most effective thank-you's are referral fees, but be very careful to see what is permitted in your jurisdiction. Several lawyers have had ethics charges filed on them for sending "investigators" to the scene of an airline accident, when the job of the investigator was actually to solicit business for the lawyer among the families of the dead and injured.

Some states allow attorneys to pay forwarding fees or referral fees to other lawyers. The referral fee is most commonly 20%, but can be higher in some kinds of personal injury cases. Often referral fees are discouraged, unethical, or illegal within a particular practice area, such as divorces.

Some lawyers are just too cheap to pay a referral fee. They may spend money on yellow pages ads, newspaper ads, and ads in the program of local arts organizations, and they think they're spending all they can afford. What they fail to realize is that the case I have just referred to them is one that they wouldn't have gotten despite all of their expenditure. Plus, a referred prospect is far more likely to become a client than a prospect from any other source, which reduces the time (expense) of convincing this prospect that she should do business with you.

If legal in your jurisdiction and ethical within your practice area, do pay a reasonable referral fee to other lawyers. But do not fall into thinking that a check takes the place of a handwritten thank-you note. It's the personal contact that will keep the referrals coming.

Be very careful with gifts to nonlawyers as a way of saying thank you for referrals. There may be specific *de minimis* guidelines in your jurisdiction. A five-dollar keychain or desktop memento may be very effective at encouraging continued referrals. A very expensive gift may get both giver and recipient in trouble.

Referrals from other professionals

Word of mouth advertising is the very best, and in many ways it's also the cheapest, but it's the most difficult to implement. And it takes a huge investment of that commodity you have the least of: your time.

Building a network of professionals who will refer business to you takes a well-thought-out campaign that is sustained and nurtured over years.

The first step is identifying the types of individuals that are in frequent contact with people who need your services. You need to be able to clearly project what's going on inside the head of your prospect, and also of your referral source. For example, a divorce lawyer may recognize that a fair number of her clients have been trying marital counseling. Naturally, it occurs to her to develop a network of marriage counselors as referral sources. But, even this is too broad. For maximum effectiveness, she needs to decide what subgroup of divorcing people she's most interested in: Christians, wives of abusers, cases with young children, cases with allegations of child abuse, etc.

Next, the attorney has to build a clear case for why she's the best attorney for this type of case, and be able to communicate it clearly to the marriage counselor. The only incentive necessary to most professionals is the confidence that their client's matter will be handled professionally.

The attorney should develop a presentation, a brochure, a device, or a gimmick that the referring professional will find useful. In our example, the attorney develops a series of seminars for marriage counselors, helping them understand the issues their clients face in a divorce, and providing continuing education for the counselors. At the seminars, the attorney hands out a booklet with information the counselor needs, such as legal terminology, steps in a divorce, and what happens next. And, the attorney develops a monthly newsletter to go to the marriage counselors to keep her name in front of them.

And then starts the hard work. The attorney goes to lots of meetings with marriage counselors, volunteers for committees of the marriage counselors' associations, writes a regular article for their newsletter, and develops personal relationships with lots of marriage counselors.

It's fairly easy to catch a fish. But it takes real work to get someone to do your fishing for you.

Attorney referral file

Attorneys like to refer clients to lawyers who refer clients to them. You will talk to a number of people who need legal services you are unable to provide, and you should always try to offer the name and telephone number of an attorney that does practice in that area.

I have found the easiest way to find lawyers to refer clients to is to enter the names of attorneys I know into my computerized telephone book, especially if they have a comparatively unique practice area. In the note area of the address book I will jot down a few key words I may wish to look for later.

For example, if I meet a lawyer who represents employees who were wrongfully terminated, I may enter "employee employer employment wrongful termination" in the note field of that attorney's record. Then, using my handheld computer or desktop I can search for the keyword and quickly find an attorney. When I give the information to the prospective client, I will always ask them to tell the new attorney, "Hal Davis sent me." I may not get a referral fee, but the other attorney will think kindly of me and may send a case my way.

This also works for other professionals. A divorce lawyer will frequently refer clients to a mortgage broker, a real estate agent, a CPA, and others. It never hurts to do a referral letter to make sure the other professional knows that the referral came from you. And, if the professionals don't refer cases to you, consider forming relationships with professionals who will.

Referrals from former clients

The most economical and most important source of referrals is your own database of former clients. Stay in touch with them. Nationwide, about 20% of the population moves each year, and forwarding orders with the post office are only effective for a few months. So, if you really want to stay in contact with your former clients, you need to mail them something more than once per year.

Your former clients do not need to be convinced what a great lawyer you are. They already know. But they do need to be reminded that you need referrals, and they need to be reminded of your areas of practice.

Learn to ask very targeted questions in seeking referrals, such as, "Who do you know at work that may be considering a divorce?" This will always produce more results than, "Who do you know that needs a lawyer?"

You should also consider a sign in your reception area that states that you are accepting referrals and you appreciate them.

Many attorneys publish a quarterly or monthly newsletter to send to their current and former clients. This can be an effective tool for staying in touch with clients, although the investment in time and money is not trivial.

There is much, much more to building referrals. The best source I have seen is *Referral Magic* by David Ward, www.time-management.com. Remember that your best tool is always to politely ask for referrals.

Run for Political Office

There are many that advise that a great way to develop name recognition to build your practice is to run for political office. I have mixed feelings about it.

In Texas, a Justice of the Peace is an elected judge that presides over small claims court and has criminal jurisdiction over matters that can be punished only by a fine, such as speeding tickets, simple assault, theft less than $50, and public intoxication. JP's are not required to be lawyers.

I ran for Justice of the Peace a few years ago and found it a very rewarding experience. Much of my campaign effort was spent going door to door introducing myself to frequent voters. Although I knocked on 3,500 doors and talked to about 2,000 people, I found less than a dozen people who were less than friendly, cordial, and receptive to me knocking on their door. I found the experience insightful and rewarding on a deeply personal level.

On the other hand, I spent several thousand dollars I could ill afford to spend in the process, and spent hundreds of hours I could have spent developing my law practice, I didn't get elected (I ran against a very popular incumbent), and I noticed no increase in my business.

My advice is never to run for political office just to build your business. Run for political office if there's a job that needs to be done and you'd like to do it, and it might have the additional blessing of building your law practice. But if you'd like to run for city council, county commissioner, or school board, you'll find that public service is rewarding indeed.

Become Recognized as an Expert

Alan Weiss is a consultant, public speaker, and author, and his book, *Million Dollar Consulting* (McGraw-Hill, 1998) advises consultants on how to take their consulting to a much higher level of revenue. When I heard him speak, someone asked him why he wrote books and booklets, and he said that he was focusing on things that "created gravity" for him. That phrase has stuck with me.

Public speakers have long ago learned that consulting, writing, and speaking create a triad of mutually supporting activities. The speaking enhances the writing and consulting, and is enhanced by the writing and consulting. Never forget that the "Counselor" part of "Attorney and Counselor" could just as well read, "Consultant."

First, of course, you must develop an area of expertise. Then, you must help your potential clients become aware that you are the expert they've needed. You do that by speaking in public and by writing a book (either one or both).

Suppose you get some work early in your career helping contractors obtain and enforce liens on residential property for the home improvement projects they have done. You find an interesting wrinkle in the law and have to do a little research. Now you're an expert. Write a brief article about what you found. Ask your contractor clients what publications they read, then contact those newsletters or magazines and offer them the article. Ask your client whether they'd like to be mentioned by name or not, and offer them reprints of the article to send to their business associates, making sure that your name and contact information is at the bottom of each article and reprint.

The newsletter will probably be receptive to another article. The trade association will probably want another speaker at their next convention, and you should agree to speak. Tape record your speech, package it, and sell it or give it to other prospective clients in the industry.

Soon you will develop a reputation as an expert and you will be the first person many people will call when they have a problem in your field.

Another approach in the same lines is becoming an expert to lawyers. Find an area of the law where other lawyers need help and make yourself helpful. If you really restrict your practice to your narrow field of expertise, lawyers will not be afraid of you stealing their clients, and they will be happy to avoid malpractice exposure. Divorce lawyers usually do not have the time and energy to keep up with retirement and tax law, so they feel uneasy about preparing Qualified Domestic Relations Orders ("QDRO's") because they tie in to federal law (ERISA). A local attorney is a frequent speaker at family law conferences telling the inside secrets and developments in this area of the law. For many people, she simply reinforces the feeling that this area of the law is too complex for the average divorce lawyer, and an expert should be used to prepare a QDRO. Who do you guess they're going to call?

For those without desire to give speeches, there is also the route of publishing a book. Even if you sell very few of them, they can be excellent for your practice. A book like the one in your hands can be printed and bound for less than $7 each in quantities as small as 300 copies, aside from the cover design and typesetting costs. Simply handing a complimentary copy to a new client or prospect will enhance your image as an expert in the area, and will help you develop your practice.

For help in becoming a speaker, I suggest you start with Dottie and Lilly Walters' book, *Speak and Grow Rich*, available from their web site at www.walters-intl.com. For help in writing and publishing a book, start with Dan Poynter's *Self-Publishing Manual*, available at www.parapublishing.com.

Chapter 5
Keeping Clients

The most important aspect of keeping clients is doing good work for them. But the client also has to know that you are working. You may be working a case very hard, but if the client hasn't heard from you in weeks, he will think you're neglecting his case.

One of the most frequent types of grievances against lawyers is that the lawyer failed to keep the client informed. There is a very simple solution. First, write a lot of letters. They do not have to be long letters, but nearly any telephone conversation should be followed up with a confirmation letter, and a copy of each letter should be sent to the client. Likewise, any paperwork you receive relating to a case should be copied and sent to the client. I had a stamp made up that says, "Client Copy: Retain for Your Records." I don't even have to write a one-sentence cover letter to send my client a copy of a document.

Recently, I've taken to scanning incoming correspondence and attaching it to an email to the client, but the result is the same. More frequent communication to your client, letting him or her know that you're still there and working for them.

Your client's file should be as thick as yours. I have had several clients who became dismayed at the lack of progress on the case, usually because it was a divorce and the client's spouse wasn't being cooperative, and my client would go see another lawyer. Inevitably, the other lawyer would look at all the copies of correspondence, pleadings, and exhibits in my client's file and then tell my client that there's nothing more that they could have done. My clients came back to me knowing that I was doing a good job. I would have lost the client if I hadn't sent my client a copy of everything.

Doing good work for clients is not enough. Eventually the engagement will end and they will begin to forget about you. You need to be sure that they will think of you whenever they need a lawyer again, and whenever they run across someone who needs a lawyer.

Make sure every your envelopes have the phrase, "Address Service Requested" below the return address, and the post office will send you a post card notifying you of any change of address.

About 25% of the population moves each year, and forwarding orders filed with the post office only remain effective for a few months. Send something, anything, to your old clients several times per year, if for no other reason than to make sure your address book remains up to date. You can send them a simple letter, a post card, a newsletter, or a small specialty advertising item. Whatever you send them must be useful, or they will stop opening your mail.

Be on the alert for information your clients want to receive. A standard Texas divorce decree will have provisions for one parent notifying the other when they would like to take summer vacation with the child. If notice is not given in writing by a certain date, default provisions kick in. I like to send a letter to all of my former divorce clients early every spring reminding them that they need to discuss summer plans with the other parent. It takes me very little time to send out this simple letter, it is greatly appreciated by my clients, I get notice of any address changes, and the client will think of me if they need modification or enforcement. While I'm at it, I can ask them if they have rewritten their will since the divorce, and ask them to be alert for friends and coworkers to refer to me.

Whenever you learn of a change in the law, think about what categories of former clients would be interested to learn about it, and send a letter, perhaps enclosing a photocopy of the statute, ruling, or newspaper article.

Specialty advertising can also be an effective way to keep your name in front of a client. Nearly any item can have your name and phone number printed on it, creating a specialty advertising item. Golf caps, shirts, coffee cups, pens, and thousands of other items are routinely used for advertising. Some lawyers like to send their clients calendars or simple refrigerator magnet versions of their business cards. With a little imagination and the assistance of a good salesman, you can come up with something interesting and inexpensive to mail to your clients that will help keep your name in front of them.

Another way to keep up with clients is telephone contact. Call up your former clients a few times each year, ask about their children, their pets, their business. Create a tickler file for client birthdays and call them or send them cards. Keep notes in your address book, so when you call them the next time you'll "remember" the previous conversation. After you have caught up with personal matters, verify their contact information (address, phone numbers, email). Don't be afraid to close by asking for some business. Ask them if they're ready to update their will. Ask them if they know anybody at work that's facing a divorce and needs a lawyer (or whatever area of practice you're trying to build).

Chapter 6
Refusing Work and Running Off Clients

It is very difficult for the new lawyer to refuse any new work, with the rent and other expenses looming. But there are certain cases and certain clients that you just can't afford to have.

First, you are ethically prohibited from accepting work unless you are competent in that area or can become competent during the engagement. Well, of course the brand new lawyer could not take any work if he had to be competent before he took it. That's one reason you want to forge friendships with experienced lawyers to talk you through your first few cases. But you do need to narrow your practice a bit or you will never be able to be competent in all the areas you practice.

I was always jealous of those lawyers who took the big fee personal injury cases. But I also recognized that it was simply one area in which I could not expect to become competent quickly enough. First, I have a strong dislike for medical terminology and anatomy, so I knew I would be limited in my ability to cross-examine doctors. Second, I had nothing in my background that made it natural to attract clients in this field, meaning that if I did get cases they would be infrequent and I would have a difficult time becoming competent.

But I also knew that personal injury lawyers always pay referral fees to referring lawyers (at least in Texas), of 20% to 33% of the total attorney's fee in the case. So, if a beautiful case happened to walk into my office, I could make a nice attorney's fee just from referring them to a lawyer who was competent. So I have refrained from taking personal injury cases.

You need to establish early on what types of cases you will be taking and which ones you will not. But I will offer some suggestions based on what kinds of cases walked through my door in the first few years I practiced.

You will see a great number of people who want a lawyer who will work for free or will take a contingent fee. Often a clearheaded analysis will reveal that while you may be able to get a technical victory, the amount of damages you are likely to be awarded are too small to be an attractive contingent fee, even if you got 100%. Beware of people wanting to sue "for the principle" because they often want you to take a contingent fee. A third of a principle will not pay the rent.

In many cases even if you win a large award, the defendant has no property and the odds of getting paid are slim to none. This lesson was driven home to me with a consumer protection case I took in my third year of practice. My client had gotten the engine rebuilt on his pickup truck and despite paying several thousand dollars for the work, the engine never worked right and the rebuilder wouldn't make it right. We finally sued under a consumer statute that allowed for treble damages plus court costs plus attorney's fees. After two days of trial it was continued for a week because of the judge's schedule, and before we could come back the rebuilder declared bankruptcy. The client got nothing, and I got nothing. The lesson: there's more to getting paid in a contingent fee case than having a meritorious case.

Libel and slander cases, or defamation as we call it in Texas, are cases where a technical victory is quite possible, but the damages are likely to be very small. If you ask the average juror what amount of money would compensate a victim for the loss of reputation suffered in the community from being called a nasty name on the sidewalk in front of the laundromat, you'll get an answer that might be as high as hundreds of dollars.

Divorces are cases where people utterly without resources may need an attorney. But if you get a reputation for doing free legal work, you'll be inundated with calls and you'll be unable to pay the rent. Many areas have a governmental agency that assists poor people with legal work. In my area it is Legal Services of North Texas, and they are funded in large part by the interest on lawyers' trust accounts. They perform a large amount of free legal work directly, but they also screen cases and refer them to lawyers in the community willing to take a free case or two. I refer people who clearly cannot afford my fees to the free legal clinic offered monthly by Legal Services of North Texas. At the clinic a legal assistant helps gather essential information on the case, and a lawyer conducts a brief interview to determine what the legal needs are and how urgent it is. After the clinic the client's finances are analyzed to see if they qualify for free legal services. Then staff calls the roster of attorneys who have volunteered to do an occasional case for free. When they call me, I always take two or three. It's good experience for me, it helps the community, and I know that the person has a genuine financial need. I also know that I am not being pressured to do more than my fair share.

Sometimes you will see a divorce client who has no access to money but is married to someone who does. Often you can take the case with no retainer and press for an early hearing to ask for interim attorney's fees to be paid by the other side. This will often work out well, but occasionally you will not be able to get those fees, and you will find yourself wrestling with the problem of withdrawing from a case when your client is helpless.

You'll get calls from folks who have an attorney in a current lawsuit, but they feel that the current attorney is not being aggressive enough, and they want someone new. But my advice is to be very careful about being the second or third lawyer on the case. Although there are bad lawyers out there, more often I run into bad clients. Clients looking for a new lawyer often have unrealistic expectations, or may simply be irrational. When you're the second lawyer, you have a higher probability of ending the case with unpaid fees, defending a grievance, or defending a malpractice suit.

There are other potential clients that may give you an uneasy feeling. If you can analyze the source of the "bad vibes," that's well and good. But trust your intuition. Some potential clients are just plain trouble waiting to happen, and no amount of good legal work on your part can save you from grief. No matter how badly you need legal work, you don't need a troublesome client.

Whatever you do, you are going to wind up with a troublesome client. My advice is to get rid of them as quickly as you can, even if it means refunding your entire fee. Even if you take the case all the way to the finish line, that will be a client you do not want to see again. When you close the file, replace the first line of their mailing address in your phone book with "REFUSE FUTURE WORK." Don't rely on your memory when they call back three years later and want help on another matter. Don't just delete them: you'll want to see them in your address book as someone to avoid. This is someone you want to refer to someone else.

There is an art to turning away work. Always give the impression that the fault is yours and that the client needs someone better. "This matter is more complex than I thought it would be, and I don't think I could do the job you deserve. In fact, I'm afraid it would be malpractice for me to take this case. I'm not going to charge you for this consultation, but I am going to give you the telephone number of a lawyer referral service. Be sure to ask for someone who is experienced in complex cases like yours." Note that this approach doesn't make the client mad with you; on the contrary, he's please that you recognized what a special person he is, and you've helped him try to find that special lawyer he deserves. Don't be so prideful that you won't say you can't handle a case – even if it's really not true, and your competence is not an issue. Stand fast in your alleged incompetence, and you'll avoid a really troublesome conversation about what you don't like about the client or the cause.

Chapter 7
Image

This chapter is mostly about the image conveyed by the written page, such as with your letterhead and business cards, by your dress, and by the location and décor of your office.

Image is *not* everything. You must be yourself, and you shouldn't try to appear to be someone else. But you should take care that your image doesn't say something you don't want to say.

I gotta be me

There are three basic approaches to image. The first is "I gotta be me," and you dress and look the way you like, and if the world doesn't like it, that's tough. Well, if that's your attitude, please go on to the next chapter, because nothing I say is going to change your mind.

Authority/Respect

But if you're interested in making your law practice a success, you are interested in the implications this has on how you dress, act, and decorate your office. The two remaining approaches to image are "respect" and "liking." Under the respect heading, you try to project an air of professionalism. Wear a suit. Wear a Rolex watch. Use lots of dark woods in your office, and fill every spare wall with law books. Buy a set of doors from the Old Bailey in London, put them on your conference room, and put a plaque by the doors telling folks where the doors came from. Whatever walls are not decorated with books should have framed copies of the U.S. Constitution, the Declaration of Independence, and a copy of Betsy Ross' first flag. Make sure you have an automobile that projects personal power (not a high-priced hotrod, but something more like a limousine).

If you project authority, then prospects will be much more likely to do what you advise. Including when you tell them to hire you.

Liking/Similarity

The third approach to projecting an image is to try to be likable, mostly through trying to appear similar to your prospects. If your prospects wear a golf shirt and jeans to the initial consultation, you should wear a golf shirt and jeans. If your prospective clients wear Timex or Casio watches, then you should leave your Rolex at home. People like to do business with people who are like them. Even aside from the question of projecting an image, you should spend the first few minutes of an initial consultation finding out something about the prospect. Find something similar between you and comment on it ("Oh, really! We go to the First Amalgamated Church also!") And find something you like about them and comment on it ("I really admire people who have tried really hard to pay their bills before trying bankruptcy.")

Blended Approach

Of course, in real life, your approach must be a blend of all three approaches. You probably can't afford all the trappings of authority, and being a good ol' boy only goes so far.

One of the most respected researchers in this field is Robert B. Cialdini, a professor at Arizona State University. His book *Influence: Science and Practice* (4ᵗʰ edition © 2001 Allyn & Bacon, Needham Heights, MA, ISBN 9-780321-011473) (www.influenceatwork.com) is a genuinely scholarly tome, written in easy-to-read language, detailing scientific studies of how people can influence others to do their bidding. It's a must-read for anybody who'll be selling anything (such as legal services).

I had a chance to hear Dr. Cialdini speak to a room full of lawyers, CPA's, and IRS Enrolled Agents about practice tips in their professional practices to influence prospects to hire them. After his speech I had a moment to talk with him and mentioned my consternation. On the one hand I should wear a suit to meet with prospects in order to project authority and garner respect. On the other hand, I should wear a golf shirt and casual slacks because that's what my prospects wear to the consultation and I should try to be like them so they'll like me. Dr. Cialdini's response was intriguing. He said that respect/authority should come first, and similarity/liking should come second. We discussed this a bit, and I mentioned that folks who came to me via my web site often comment on how informative my web site is. I also said that I usually send a big packet of information to folks before they come for their first consultation. We agreed that my web site and advance information would serve the respect/authority function, and that when my clients and I met face to face, I should focus on being similar/likeable, and should dress like them.

Scarcity

Something is more valuable when it is rarer. A first edition of a Dickens novel is worth a fortune, even though it contains the same information as a cheap paperback at the used book store. Always project an air of being in demand. When someone asks you how your practice is going, the best answer is, "Great!" If someone asks for an appointment, don't say, "Pick a time, there's nothing on my schedule." Instead, say, "I have an opening at 3:30 on Wednesday. Would that be convenient?" You don't want prospective clients wondering why nobody wants to hire you.

This appears shallow at first, but there's more to it. You'll get the respect you demand, not what you deserve. You're a high-priced expert, and your clients and prospects should not expect to reach you on a Sunday afternoon or Tuesday evening. Don't make it a practice of giving out your cell phone number. In most situations, there's nothing you can do until your office opens Monday morning. And remember, you want your clients to respect you enough to expect to pay for your time. They might think that if they call you on Saturday afternoon, there's no way they'd have to pay for the call. Demand your clients respect your time, and you'll increase the chance they'll pay their bills.

If you're doing well enough to afford an assistant, so much the better. They need to be your gatekeeper, keeping people from stealing the only thing you have to sell: your time. Besides, a really good assistant can sell you much better than you can sell yourself.

Your image in print

Everything a client or prospective client sees with your name on it conveys a message beyond the actual words. The typefaces (fonts) you use, the way words are arranged on the page, and your use of other graphical elements all combine to say something. Do not confuse people by having a business card that looks nothing like your letterhead, or a web page that looks completely different from your ad in the church newspaper.

The first step is to design a letterhead and a business card that are clear and project the desired image. There are a number of books that will help you in this process, and some of the ones that have helped me are *Using Type Right* by Philip Brady; *Type from the Desktop* by Clifford Burke; *Desktop Publisher's Easy Type Guide*; *Type Design, Color, Character & Use* by Michael Beaumont; and *The Hammermill Guide to Desktop Publishing in Business* by Bruce McKenzie.

Typefaces

After you have done some study, find some typefaces you like and think about the type of image you'd like to project. Then I suggest you consult with a graphic artist to get a design that says what you want to say. Keep in mind that you want flexibility. You'll want to use the same basic design for letterhead, envelopes, business cards, and advertising.

I don't have professionally printed stationery. I buy high quality paper, but I load my letterhead information into my word processor so that it automatically appears when I write a letter. Not only is this less expensive than professionally printed stationery, but it allows me to readily update my address or other information, and gives me something to work from if I want to use the same image to create an ad or post card.

While a couple of different typefaces can be used on one piece harmoniously, be very careful not to make your letterhead look like a ransom note. You can use a highly decorative typeface sparingly, but remember that it must be legible or it fails to achieve its purpose. It's also a good idea to keep all the typefaces within a certain family to achieve a unified image. Although dozens of typefaces come with your computer's operating system and software, don't be afraid to get a catalog from a company that sells typefaces and pick out a typeface or two that will set you apart from the crowd.

> I'm really tired of Times New Roman. I think it is overused and ugly. The advantage is that it is very legible, but it was not designed for correspondence. As the name implies, it was designed for a newspaper so that it would look good and be legible in very small sizes, in narrow columns, tightly packed. This paragraph is set in Times New Roman.

There are many typefaces that are as businesslike and legible as Times New Roman and are much more interesting and attractive. Just a few to consider are Bookman, Garamond,

Bembo, Caslon, Goudy Old Style, Baskerville, Perpetua, and Palatino.

I recommend that you consider using a typeface that is a bit unusual (*i.e.,* other than Times Roman) for another reason. Sometimes it's nice to be able to tell at a glance whether a document you have emailed to your client has been altered before they printed it out and signed it. So, sometimes it's worth the effort to purchase a typeface that doesn't just come with your computer's operating system or software.

I recommend you stay away from highly ornate typefaces, simply because they are very difficult to read, especially when they have been photocopied a couple of generations, or have been faxed a couple of times.

I also recommend you stay away from san-serif typefaces, because they are more difficult to read. Serifs are the little "hooks" on the ends of the letters. They hook the eye into following the shape, and make text easier to read. San serif fonts don't have the serifs ("san" meaning "without"). The first letter below is in a serifed font, and the second is in a san-serif font.

This paragraph is done in a san serif typeface (Arial). Many graphic artists prefer san serif fonts for many applications because they believe it projects a more modern, "cleaner" look. That may be true. But when I see long stretches of text set in a san serif font, I find it much more difficult to read.

Chapter 8
Staff

In this chapter I hope to show you that you really can't afford staff, at least not initially; that you really can manage your office without staff; and that when it's time to add staff you really need the experience of having done without staff.

In 2002 in Dallas, Texas competent, trained legal secretaries were routinely commanding salaries in excess of $40,000 per year. Experienced paralegals and really good legal secretaries were making considerably more. While lawyers graduating at the top of their class going to work for large firms were making $100,000 plus, a great many lawyers just embarking on a solo career are very concerned that they will not be able to earn $40,000 their first year. Given the benefits and payroll taxes that would have to be paid for a secretary, as well as the additional rent and computer equipment needs that a secretary would require, a lawyer trying to build his practice could easily find himself to committing to a salary in excess of what would be left over to pay the lawyer.

Don't even consider starting a solo law practice with a brand-new secretary or paralegal. You don't know enough to train them, and you can't afford to be liable for their blunders.

Sharing a secretary is usually a bad idea as well. Jesus said that a man cannot serve two masters, for he will love one and despise the other. I've seen it happen with secretaries. One lawyer will wind up paying half the costs but wind up with much less than half of the secretary's work and loyalty. And inevitably the secretary will answer the phone and direct the new client to the lawyer she likes best, rather than the one who paid for the advertising to make the phone ring.

But at no time in history has it been as easy to practice law without a secretary as it is now. Reliable, inexpensive voice mail systems have become so accepted that many callers wince at leaving a message with a real human because they know the message will be botched. Document assembly programs and forms on disk have rendered obsolete the need for blindingly fast typists to simply transcribe forms from one document to another.

Anyone who can pass a bar exam can surely teach herself to touch type. No real speed is necessary; you just need to be able to type without looking at your fingers. Once that threshold is crossed, you will be able to type almost as fast as you can compose legalese in your mind. If you really have trouble typing and are convinced you can't learn, voice recognition systems are available to allow you to dictate to your computer.

But most legal writing is not about writing page after page from scratch. It's about taking somebody else's form, or the form you used last week, and adding a paragraph, deleting a paragraph, moving a paragraph around, and filling in the blanks with different information. This does not require any great typing facility.

Most lawyers who have made a real effort to do without a secretary have found that it is more efficient for the lawyer to simply change the document himself. There is simply too much lawyer time involved in describing changes to someone else, and then checking to see that the changes were done correctly, without even considering the cost of the secretary's time.

Some lawyers have a hard time adopting technology. My strong advice is to get over it. Technology is your friend. Use it.

One of the great books I read in undergraduate school (I minored in sociology) was *Future Shock* by Alvin Tofler. Mr. Tofler points out that the technology has led to an increasing rate of change, and thus change itself is something to come to grips with. He puts forth the proposition that there are two types of folks in our society: those that embrace technology, that love technology, and that long for new uses of technology, and those who fall behind, throw up their hands, and say, "I can't keep up." The first group uses the advantages of technology to make their lives easier. The second group opts out of the mainstream and becomes spectators.

I believe Benjamin Franklin said, "Whether you think you can, or think you cannot, you are right." That is particularly appropriate for the lawyer trying to practice law using technology instead of staff. A good, strong, "I think I can," goes a long way in trying to figure out how to get things done quickly and economically. But if you are convinced that you cannot make technology work for you, then you need to hire extremely trustworthy staff to run your business life for you.

As your practice grows, you may find that there are certain tasks that you would rather have someone else do, and you'll be able to afford to hire someone else to do them. The test is whether you are so busy that doing the low-value task (typing, stuffing envelopes, etc.) prevents you from doing a high-value task (meeting with prospective clients, designing your next advertising campaign, etc.). Try to use part-time personnel because you don't pay for benefits, and you don't pay when they don't work (sick days, vacations). University and community college placement offices and bulletin boards are great places to get part-time personnel.

Get your take-home pay into the vicinity of six figures before you consider adding permanent full-time staff. When you do, providing you have sufficient work to keep both of you busy, you will find that the secretary can be a profit center. The secretary should be able to command a billing rate about a quarter to a third of yours, and should bill any time spent answering client inquiries or preparing documents for a client. Clients will quickly learn that they can get their questions answered for lower cost by speaking with the secretary, freeing up your time and still making you money.

Finally, one simply cannot supervise a worker when she doesn't know how to do the worker's job. You will lose your license if you don't handle your trust account properly, and you can't train someone else in the procedure until you know how to do it yourself. You will lose business if your secretary doesn't answer the phone the way you want it answered.

Staff come and go, and when it's time to replace staff, or simply to hire a temporary, you'll be the one teaching the person how to do his job.

When you are ready to add staff, I suggest you take the time to prepare an employee handbook. You need to spell out all the basics for the new employee, from how you want the phone answered, to how you want the new appointment entered into the calendar, to the format for correspondence, to where to file the letter in the computer. Taking the time to write all this down will give the secretary greater confidence, and will save you a great deal of time when the secretary is sick and you call in a temporary.

Chapter 9
Where to Office

The two aspects of Where to Office are picking a city, and picking an office.

What city? What part of town?

Picking a metropolitan area in which to office will usually be a function of factors other than market demographics. Most people will want to build their professional lives in the same area in which they have built their lives before now. Your relatives and high school friends will be an important source of your first clients, both directly and as referral sources. Certainly those who had a career before going to law school will want to remain in close contact with those they knew from a previous professional life. Do not abandon your home turf lightly.

Having said that, if you grew up in a small town or if your hometown is in decay (or both), then your prospects may only be acceptable in a new location. Pick the best possible combination of already knowing people in the city and finding a city with prosperity.

I am a fourth-generation Dallasite, so it was a forgone conclusion that I would be practicing law somewhere in the greater Dallas area. Fortunately, Dallas has generally prospered over the last several decades, so I did not have to wrestle with the prospect of relocation. But the Dallas / Fort Worth Metroplex covers thousands of square miles, probably a dozen cities with populations of at least 100,000, and over a dozen counties. How was I to pick a specific market in that area?

Fortunately, I came to the law from a consulting background, and one of the things I did right was to do a demographic analysis of the area. First, I researched a number of demographic factors for each county in the area. I simply went to the library's business and commerce section and asked a librarian for help. We decided some good factors to consider were:

- Sales tax revenue. While not a perfect measure, it would serve as a measure of the local economic engine. With enough money flowing around, surely some would be available for me to earn.

- Population and population growth.

- Number of housing starts. A good measure of whether people are moving to the area.

- Commercial construction start dollars. Clearly, one commercial construction start is not the same as another. To adjust for size, commercial construction starts are often stated in terms of the total amount expected to be spent on the project. This is a measure of how attractive businesses are finding the area.

- Number of lawyers. I went to a law library and got a Martindale-Hubbell Law Directory, which is a phone book of lawyers for lawyers. I went to the section where there is no advertising and I counted the number of lawyers listed on a sample page. Then I counted the number of pages of lawyers in each county and estimated the number of lawyers in each county.

I divided each of my economic factors by the number of lawyers in the county to wind up with prosperity, size, and growth factors *per lawyer* for each county. I cast my lot with Collin County, which is just north of Dallas, and I have never looked back. It is not terribly important which growth factors you choose to analyze, but you owe it to yourself to apply some analysis to the market that you hope will feed you for the next forty years or so.

What part of town?

It may be hard for a lawyer first starting out to do this, but it's worth a try. In order to figure out what neighborhood to put your office in, it really helps to have a clear idea of who your prospective clients are, and how they'll come to see you.

- If your prospective clients tend to be dependent on public transportation, a location close to a commuter rail station would be a good choice.

- If your prospective clients are doctors, then maybe your office should be across the street from the hospital.

- If your prospective clients are businesses downtown, your office should be downtown.

- If your prospective clients are affluent housewives, your office should be in a zip code with expensive houses.

Choosing an office environment

There are a number of options for choosing an office for the new lawyer. Some are very lonely, such as leasing your own space in a commercial or retail building, or even officing from home. Some are more social, such as officing with other attorneys.

Much of your revenue the first year will be contract work for other lawyers, or it will be referrals. Many lawyers have more work than they can accomplish. With a little pleasant arm twisting, most will be able to pull a folder from the bottom of their inbox and find a job for you to do for $50 per hour or so. The lawyer will review the work and bill the client several times the amount. You will have earned an honest wage, the client will have received a quality product, and the other lawyer will have gotten something out of his inbox at a nice profit to him.

Other lawyers will have clients that cannot afford to pay their high rates and will refer them to you on the expectation that you can do very well on a much lower rate. Often they will expect a referral fee, and often that will be the appropriate thing to do (check the regulations in your state). You'll earn $100 per hour or so, and the referring lawyer may earn $20 per hour just for thinking of you.

Sometimes you will have a puzzling situation and you'll want to ask the advice of a lawyer who has been around the block.

Unless your timing is really bad, the other lawyer will be flattered to be asked.

Often you'll want to go to lunch with people that are fun to talk with. Lawyers are much maligned by society today, but I have always found it interesting to converse with people who are self employed, well educated, and have enough showbiz in them to address a jury.

These benefits can all be obtained by finding a group of lawyers who have a spare office for rent. Look around, evaluate your options, and ask about the reputation of the lawyers in each group.

The easiest way to find an office-sharing deal in a suburb of 200,000 or less is to get out the Martindale-Hubbell Law Directory again, and look for addresses where there are several attorneys. Unless you are in a downtown area, you will probably find lots of solos, lots of firms of five or fewer attorneys, and very few locations (not necessarily firms) with more than five attorneys. Often a firm will share office space with solos, or even with another partnership.

Having identified the addresses where there are groups of lawyers, you drive to the building, look on the building directory, and then go introduce yourself to the lawyer in charge of the suite (tell the receptionist you're a lawyer interested in office space and ask who you should talk to). Explain your situation, chat with the lawyer, and ask about available office space in town. Even if there is space available, ask about other space in town, as you'll want a little gossip about which lawyers would cast a favorable reflection on you by association.

If you find space available, ask the hard questions. How much contract work could I expect? How much in the way of referrals? Are referral fees customary, and how much? Do you often go to lunch in groups? Would you mind if I occasionally dropped by your office with a legal issue that's puzzling me? How much is rent? When is your lease up? Before I decide, could we all get together for a barbecue so my spouse can meet you, your spouse, and the other attorneys and spouses?

Law school buddies are often tempted to form a partnership. This is usually a mistake. Two neophytes may find a partnership an opportunity to starve together. You'll want to start with an environment where there is more work than can be done, and hope that a large portion finds its way to your inbox.

If and when you do decide to form a partnership, you will probably find that diversity will work in your favor. Every lawyer will find friends and relatives asking them about an area of the law about which the lawyer is relatively ignorant. If the lawyer has a partner to refer this work to, then everybody benefits. The client is referred to a competent attorney, the referring attorney gets some sort of referral fee through the partnership, and the referred attorney gets work.

Many lawyers have found it profitable to find office space in an executive suite. A suite is divided into a number of small offices, with one shared conference room, one shared reception area, and one shared receptionist. A lawyer may find herself with an office between a building contractor and an insurance agent, with a lobbyist across the hall. While there may be fewer opportunities to get advice from older lawyers, there may be more opportunities for legal work with the business folk in the suite.

This brings me to some advice that I will repeat in a later chapter, but it cannot be overemphasized:

Own your telephone number.

In any office-sharing environment, either with a law firm or in an executive suite, your telephone line may go through a receptionist's board. Make it very clear, in writing, that your telephone line is your telephone line, and when you leave the suite you will take your telephone number with you. When law firms break up, the biggest acrimony will be over who keeps the telephone number.

You can always explain to your clients that your address has changed. But if an old client calls the number he had for you and another lawyer answers, the odds are very good that your client has a new lawyer.

Do not let a law firm or executive suite handle your relationship with the telephone company. Call the telephone company yourself to order a telephone number, and then ask them to coordinate the installation with the office manager. If you later find yourself moving across the city and the telephone company tells you that you cannot keep the same telephone number, keep asking until you get the right answer. If no arrangement can be made to make that old number ring in your new place, then don't move. Or rent a closet in your old building, install the phone there, and then forward the phone to your new location.

Back to office sharing arrangements. For those who need to keep operating expenses to the bare minimum, there is a cost-effective way to office from home while putting on a more prosperous appearance. Often a lawyer will allow another lawyer to put her shingle outside the door, use the conference room occasionally, and use the law library while the junior lawyer actually offices at home, for only a hundred dollars or so per month. Once again, check into the reputation of the folks you office with, or even appear to office with.

Eventually you may wish to rent your own space directly from a landlord. You'll need to know a few basics about the different types of leases. Of course you'll want to read the lease carefully, and you shouldn't be afraid to ask the advice of an attorney that handles commercial and lease transactions on a regular basis.

Commercial and retail leases are quite different. Commercial leases are the leases you will encounter in the typical office building. You will pay a certain dollar amount per square foot leased per year, and this figure will include the electricity, heating, air conditioning, and someone coming through your office daily to vacuum and empty the trash. There may be a Common Area Maintenance charge to pass on the shared expenses, such as the maintenance on elevators, utilities to the bathrooms, and other expenses not attributable to a particular suite. Many commercial tenants do not realize that when the landlord wallpapers and carpets the hallway that each tenant's "rent" will go up because of the expenses that are passed on.

Retail leases are usually for storefronts. The advantage to the lawyer is that members of the public driving or walking by will see that there is a lawyer here, and may even see the lawyer's name. This may be less valuable than it first appears, because you will probably get very little new business from passers-by seeing the word "lawyer" on the front of the building (unless your professional rules allow you to advertise a trade name or area of practice, such as "Workplace Injury Lawyer").

As a general rule, retail space is more expensive than commercial space. A retail lease will typically provide a place where the tenant can build and maintain his own mini-building. While the landlord may warrant that the roof will not leak, anything else within the space is the tenant's responsibility. The tenant will pay all utilities, will call the plumber at his own expense if the toilet stops working, and will have to replace the air conditioning unit when it stops working. Quoted on a per-square-foot basis, retail space may seem attractive compared to commercial space. But you'll need a much more detailed comparison before you can make a decision on retail versus commercial space.

Chapter 10
Telephony

The number one way you will get new business is from people calling you. You must have a telephone number that does not change. Make sure that when you enter a partnership, an office-sharing arrangement, or an executive suite that you have it in writing that when the arrangement ends you still own the telephone number you had at the start. If that number is answered by another lawyer, your client has a new lawyer. The best advice is for you to contact the telephone company directly to order a telephone line.

I plan to update this book annually, but the field of telephones and Internet access is changing so rapidly that it is likely to be outdated very soon after publication. Nonetheless, this is information you need to have to set up your office.

Do not concern yourself with adopting the latest technology simply because it is the latest technology. You need proven technology that will allow you to get your work done without interruption. If newer technology offers advantages you need, consider adopting it. But recognize that the newer the technology you are adopting, the greater the problems you will have finding competent assistance.

A basic arrangement

You want to make sure that someone calling your number will never get a busy signal, and the call will never go unanswered. Your absolute minimum configuration will be two telephone lines and a pager with voice mail associated with it. When you're in the office, you'll make all of your outgoing telephone calls on the second line, and you will also use it for faxes (and for a computer data line, if you can't get internet access any way except dial-up). You'll set up your first line with call forward busy/no answer to forward to your pager number. If you don't answer a call on the first line (call forward — no answer), or if someone calls while you're on that line (call forward — busy), the call rolls over to the pager where they leave a message and then you are paged. You'll publish the second phone number as your fax line. You need to be sure that your pager can be set to vibrate instead of beep so that you can use it even when you're in court.

You will need a good answering machine.

A more flexible arrangement

The above configuration will work well for the one-person office, but a more expensive system will offer more options.

As you become busier, it will be more of an inconvenience to tie up your fax line (which is also your outgoing voice line) with a dial-up connection to the internet. The first thought is to get another telephone line. But often for about the same price you can get high-speed always-on internet access. DSL service will use the actual copper wiring of one of your existing lines, but will use the higher-frequency part that is not used for voice or fax communication, effectively getting a voice line and a data line on one wire.

DSL service is only available within a certain number of feet of the local telephone switching office, so it may not be available in your location. There are other options.

- Perhaps your office building or the executive suites you are using will have purchased a high-speed data line and will allow you to share access to it via a local network for a reasonable fee.

- Your local cable television provider may have run cable to your building, and you may be able to get access to the internet through a cable modem.

- If your building will permit you to put a mini satellite dish on the roof or side of your building, you may be able to get high-speed internet access through one of the satellite television providers.

- In a few markets, microwave or radio access to internet providers is available.

In most major metropolitan areas there is a free monthly newspaper with articles on computers and technology, and it will be full of ads for internet service providers. The publication may even have a comparison guide to internet service providers, which may be constantly updated on their web site.

Fax

It is tempting for the computer-savvy consumer to view fax as dinosaur technology, and to shun it. Don't. I'm sending emails to other lawyers much more frequently, but the vast majority of quick written communication with other lawyers is via fax, and will remain so for the foreseeable future.

There are systems that allow you to use your computer as an incoming fax machine, but I generally do not recommend them for the same reasons that I do not recommend using your computer as an answering machine. You can't afford to have your system go down and then miss a fax.

Using fax software to allow your computer to send faxes is another matter. This is a very convenient way of sending a fax, and will produce very clean output on the other end, but it does have a couple of problems. First, you can only send documents that are in your computer. You cannot transmit pieces of paper that are in your file, unless you get a scanner, and that adds a whole level of complexity to the situation. Second, for the same reason, you can't really send a signed document or letter. There are workarounds, but they are clumsy. Using your computer as an outgoing fax machine is a convenient way of getting draft documents to your client.

You will need a fax machine, or at least access to one, for sending faxes.

There are several services that allow you to receive incoming faxes as attachments to email. See www.j2.com. I have used this service off and on for several years. The advantages are that you can receive your faxes wherever you take a laptop computer, and you can easily forward faxes you receive to your client as an email attachment. But recently I've had trouble with the attachments being corrupted somewhere along the way and I've been unable to read the fax. I've been forced to send a fax to the sending number and ask them to resend to a real fax machine. Try email fax if you like, and if it stops working, redirect your faxes to your real fax machine. My advice about never changing your phone number does not apply to fax numbers. I've changed fax numbers several times and I don't think I've lost any new business because of it.

Mobile telephone

If you expect that you will be out of the office a fair amount of the time, I recommend that you buy a mobile telephone. Make sure you can easily, quickly (and silently!) turn off the ringer and put it in vibrate mode. Recently I've noticed that some of the cuter-sounding telephones played tunes as they are being switched off or placed into silent mode. Imagine yourself in the courtroom and you hear somebody else's phone go off. As the bailiff marches to the offender to confiscate a phone, you realize that you haven't silenced your phone. Do you just hope it doesn't ring, or do you turn it off, knowing it will play a dying ditty?

Set up your main telephone line with call forwarding busy/no answer to your mobile phone. Allow yourself the freedom of not answering the mobile phone every time it rings. When you are in another conversation or when you are driving, at least you are immediately notified that you have received a call and you can return it as soon as you have a moment.

Another little tip. Every cell phone I've seen has a single button you can push when a phone call is coming in which will stop the ringing without answering the call. There will be times when it's not convenient to answer the phone, and you don't want to let it ring 4 or 5 times before it rolls over to voice mail. Read the manual, and find out how to send the call directly to voice mail.

Having a mobile telephone will allow you to provide superior customer service. First, if your phone rings at a time and place where you are able to take the call, you've saved that caller from voice mail. Second, if you are unable to take the call and they leave a message on voice mail, at least when you are able to pick up messages and return calls you will not have the delay of finding a telephone to use.

And now a story I just can't leave out. Two days after the terrorist attacks on New York City on September 11, 2001, I was at a morning devotional and prayer service. It was a fairly big church, and it was packed. Standing room only. I bet there were 3,000 people there. Two or three television news trucks were at the church with camera crews inside. There were several stirring speeches, a couple of wonderful musical performances, and then a minute of silent prayer. You guessed it: 10 seconds into the minute of silent prayer, a cell phone went off. It rang twice before the owner realized that he had to stop it from ringing. Sure, he should have put it on "silent" before he came in, but he didn't. Apparently the owner had not read the manual and learned how to send the call directly to voice mail. But 20 seconds into the minute of silence, he chose to actually answer the call. Now, to his credit, he didn't use the cell phone voice, where one talks three times as loudly as you do without a phone stuck to your head. But there was a mumbled, "Let me call you back. ... Yeah....Yeah... Bye." But the *coup de grace* was when he disconnected and powered off ... and his phone played a precious little dying melody. The lessons: (1) try to remember to put your phone on silent mode before you go into a meeting; (2) learn how to make the phone stop ringing and send the caller to voice mail without answering the phone; and (3) learn how to turn your phone off or put it in silent mode without making a lot of noise in the process.

Remote Call Forwarding

If you have a mobile telephone, you should also have remote call forwarding installed on your main telephone line. This allows you to forward your office telephone, even when you are not in the office. This gives you the freedom to wander the town doing errands, chatting up prospects, meeting clients, or doing volunteer work with the assurance that you will not miss important telephone calls.

I will often be in court in the morning, but I am often out by mid-morning. Upon leaving the courthouse I will use my mobile phone to remotely forward my office calls to my mobile phone. Throughout the day, until I return to the office, I will take telephone calls if it is convenient, and if it is not convenient, I'll let my mobile phone's voice mail pick up the call and I'll return the call shortly. When I return to the office, or at the end of the business day, or if I go back into court in the afternoon, I'll unforward my calls and let the voice mail system at the office pick them up. Then, my cell phone will ring (or vibrate) only if someone leaves an urgent message for me, or if someone calls the office when the answering machine is taking another call.

Digital messaging

There are a number of devices that allow digital messaging, through a mobile phone, through a handheld computer, or a digital pager. Telephones and most pagers use Short Messaging Service, or SMS, which is limited to about 150 characters. The good news is that you are immediately notified when you receive such a message, by beep or vibration. The bad news is that your sender has to have some sort of keyboard to send the message, and the message must be very brief.

Increasingly, phones and pocket computers are being made available with wireless email capability. The good news is that considerably longer messages can be sent and received. The bad news is that you are not automatically notified when you have received an email. SMS and wireless email can be used together harmoniously.

If you have a web site, you probably have the capability to control your own email service, and can have several email addresses. You can set up a group addresses, such as emergency@yourdomain.com. When the email system gets an email addressed to emergency@yourdomain.com, it can resend the email to both your SMS address on your phone, and to the email address of your wireless device. The SMS message will be too short to give you any useful information, except to tell you to check your email. Then, you check your email and get the complete information.

This may be a very useful approach if you have an answering service or a receptionist who'll send you an email when you get a message. You may want to provide this information to a select few clients.

Someone sending you a message can use their computer to type in an extremely brief message (often 80 characters or less). Clients or prospective clients will find it is less hassle to simply leave a voice message for you. Most secretarial services will type in "PLS CALL JOHN JACOBS AT 555-123-4567" which is not really any more useful than a voice mail message, or simply the telephone number on a pager. I have been unable to get a secretarial service to put more useful information in the page, such as "BROTHER ARRESTED: JOHN JACOBS 555-123-4567" or "NEEDS PROT ORDER: JOHN JACOBS 555-123-4567."

As you do not have a secretary or a teammate, I predict that the most useful information you will receive with this technology is "PLS BUY MILK AND EGGS ON WAY HOME." This is something that just as easily could have been done with a voice mail message. If your clients have an urgent message for you, they will call and have you paged.

But if you hire a competent secretary, you may have a realistic use for text messaging.

Internet Access and Web Site Hosting

Just as you want your own telephone number that will follow you wherever you go, you will also want a web site address (URL) and an email address that follow you. This is done by getting a domain. Think of it as a vanity license plate that must be unique in all the world but allows more than seven characters. The fee for registering the site is usually less than $30 per year, and your web host will probably take care of the details for you.

Although you will probably find those who will take care of everything for you, from Internet access to hosting your web site to designing and implementing your site, I have found that I get better service at a fair price if I break the services up. I have an Internet service provider whose only job is to get me connected quickly, reliably, and inexpensively. If they fall down on the job, they're fired with no disruption. I have another service hosting my web site and handling my email, and they provide much better service and statistics on my web site than I ever got from an all-in-one provider. And lastly, I originally chose local people I know from the chamber of commerce to design my web site. They know that if they do a lousy job the whole chamber of commerce is going to know about it.

You can find Internet access providers in the free newspapers about computers available in the entrance lobbies of the big local bookstores. You can find web hosting services in the same place, as well as in the back of better computer magazines. Web site designers you should meet through your local chamber of commerce.

Do not give a web site designer a blank check. Go on the Internet, look for lawyers, and decide what you like and don't like about various lawyer web sites. Sketch what features and appearance you want your web site to have. Then talk to the site designer.

If you are able to type without looking at the keys, if you learn new software fairly quickly, and if you're not trying to do anything particularly fancy with your web site, consider building and maintaining your own web site. Sometimes I'll get a call or email from a client or a prospect asking a question that I realize should have been addressed on my web site. I like being able to quickly add the paragraph or two and update the web site in less than five minutes. It would have taken considerably longer than that to explain the change to a web developer, and probably another several days before the change was activated on my site.

As I write this, the *de facto* standard for building and maintaining your own web site is Microsoft Front Page. If your goal is simply to present information, you'll find it easy enough to use, quick enough to learn, and flexible and powerful enough. But if you're considering going this direction, keep it in mind when you select your web host. They will need to have proper software installed at their end to allow your software to have maximum flexibility, power, and ease of use. In this case, you would ask the host if they have Front Page Extensions installed, whether there's an additional charge for that software, and what version they have.

A final note on web pages. A recent fad is the "flash" or "splash" page. When you type in the address of the firm you're looking for, you are treated to something colorful and graphically interesting, but which doesn't actually convey any useful information. After the hoopla, you'll see something that says, "click here to enter," and you can then begin to find the information you were originally looking for. Flash pages were designed by web designers to help them build a resume of what they can do. Your clients will not like them, especially if they're surfing the net from a dial-up connection, and it takes a while to load the flash page. Remember: the average web surfer takes about 5 seconds to look at a web page and decide whether to investigate further or go to another site.

Cordless telephones and confidentiality

Cordless telephones can be very handy about the office, especially now that they are available with inexpensive headsets. You can be free to wander the hallways in your suite and talk with other attorneys knowing that if a potential client calls you will not miss it. I also like using a headset for all of my calls at the office, and it's easier and less expensive to find a headset for a cordless phone than for a wired phone.

But anytime you use a telephone that is not hard-wired, including a cellular telephone, remember you are broadcasting to anybody who is in range of your transmitter. Cellular telephone and cordless telephones are very easy to intercept, by pranksters, by casual snoops, by serious investigators, and by government agents. Consider that police do not need a wiretap warrant to monitor your cordless telephones because the U.S. Supreme Court has ruled that there is no expectation of privacy in cellular/cordless telephone calls (if you wanted privacy, why would you broadcast the conversation in the public's radio spectrum?).

Later digital technology in both mobile phones and in cordless phones increases clarity, range, battery life, and privacy. Digital transmissions are harder to snoop on, and even harder to accidentally overhear. But a determined snoop will overhear your wireless conversations and if that is a concern, you should not use cordless phones. You should also have a professional sweep your office for bugs periodically. Personally, I have no secrets, and none of my clients is so high profile that I'm concerned about snooping. But each lawyer should make her own decision.

Chapter 11
Furniture and Fixtures

What could be less exciting than furniture and fixtures? Well, maybe so, but you will be buying some, and you might appreciate the words of someone who has gone before.

Many lawyers envision themselves behind a big shiny desk, with the client seated on the other side. The client has his hat in his hands, and the lawyer is leaned back, deep in thought, with his fingers steepled across his midsection. That's how you earn the big bucks: looking thoughtful and earnest. It is also contrary to my recommendations.

You will be thought a greater lawyer if you are thought to be a good listener. After all, how can you solve someone's problem unless you understand it? I do not think that 28 square feet of polished mahogany between lawyer and client leads to a warm fuzzy feeling on the client's part.

If you can swing it, get an office big enough for a small circular conference table and four chairs. Do this even if it means skimping on the size of your desk, or even doing without a desk in the traditional sense. When you counsel a client or potential client, take two seats that are beside each other (not opposite each other) and turn them to face each other. That is, 12 o'clock facing the chair at 3 o'clock, not the one at 6 o'clock. Invite the client to one and you take the other. That way there's a table for spreading out papers, but there's no barrier between you and the client.

In addition to the four side chairs for the small conference table, you will need one or two more chairs. One will be an ergonomic desk chair for you to sit in while you work at your computer. The other is a lightweight utility chair, such as a folding chair, a ladderback, or a bentwood, whatever fits with your décor. This chair is for the fifth person when a couple comes in to sign wills. In Texas, a will needs two witnesses and a notary, so if a married couple is the client and the lawyer serves as a witness or notary, there are five people at the table. Adjust for your state's rules. And while it's preferable for the lawyer to be neither a notary nor a witness, I've never been in an office where there was an abundance of witnesses and notaries.

Standardize your paperwork on letter-sized paper right from the start. Legal sized paper is hardly used anymore, and if you do get handed some, you can fold the bottom up or you can reduce it on the photocopier. Everything will be cheaper and more manageable if your files, filing cabinets, and paper are all letter-sized from the start.

You will want two filing cabinets. If you have a desk, the filing space in it will probably be too small to be of any use. You will want an attractive, wood two-drawer lateral file where you can reach it without getting out of your computer chair. That's where you'll keep your active files, along with files of this year's consultations and the files of bills you have paid (sorted by category for when the IRS audits you).

The second filing cabinet is a four or five drawer lateral filing cabinet that will hold a couple of years' worth of closed files. After files have been closed for a couple of years you will transfer the files to cardboard boxes and put them in storage.

Recently, I've changed my mind on the filing cabinet business. First, I found a "tub" that can hold all my active files, and I can get to them without opening a drawer. Second, I bought a scanner and I'm now going paperless on my closed files. So, aside from my open files, all I need is filing space for my paid bills, the warranty on the answering machine, last year's malpractice insurance application, etc.

You will need a worktable. It should be at the proper height for a computer keyboard, and this is where most of your work will get done. There should be room to spread out the papers you are looking at while you type. I don't have a traditional desk. Just the worktable and the client interview table.

You will need a few bookshelves. Part of them will hold the nice looking law books that are part of the image of practicing law. The rest will hold the real notebooks, dictionaries, and paper bound law books that you actually use.

I don't think you'll want a postage meter. They cost too much, and if you don't like using stamps you can use the Internet to print postage using your printer. See www.estamp.com, www.stamps.com, and www.endicia.com.

Personally, I keep a very messy desk. I have a large one-room office, and I've put a cubicle partition between my working desk (messy) and my conference table (neat).

Credit card terminal

If you provide legal services to individuals (as opposed to businesses) you will want to accept credit cards. The discount because of the fees is not significant compared to the increase in business you should see. And you'll want to get signage within your office with the logos of credit card companies.

> "… college students were willing to spend an average of 29% more money for mail-order catalog items when they examined the items in a room that contained MasterCard insignias; moreover, they had no awareness that the credit card insignias were part of the experiment. A final study showed that when asked to contribute to a charity (the United Way), college students were markedly more likely to give money if the room they were in contained MasterCard insignias than if it did not (87 percent versus 33 percent). … Even though credit cards themselves were not used for the charity donation, the mere presence of their symbol (with its attendant positive associations) spurred people to spend more cash." (Cialdini, *Influence: Science and Practice, 4th Ed.,* p. 164) (www.influenceatwork.com).

There are three basic options for processing credit cards.

- You can set up a merchant account where you process a paper charge form, have the client sign it, and call an automated telephone service to verify that there is "room" on the credit card for the charge (and that the card isn't stolen, etc.). This requires the most human intervention, as you have to batch up your tickets and prepare a deposit slip to your checking account.

- You can lease or buy a terminal such as the ones in most retail stores, where you swipe the card, punch in the amount of the charge, then the terminal dials the service, verifies the charge, handles processing the charge to your account, hangs up, and then prints something for your client to sign. This scheme results in the lowest discount rates, and pretty low per-transaction charges, but you do have to pay a monthly charge for the use of the terminal. The discounts are lower because you swipe the card, proving that you actually have the card in your possession and that the info on the front of the card matches what's on the magnetic stripe, which dramatically reduces the risk that the transaction is fraudulent or that the card is counterfeit or stolen.

- Then there's the "virtual terminal" where your service simply gives you access to a web page that you fill out and submit the charge over the internet. The online form will look exactly like what you'd fill out for an online purchase. Discounts are slightly higher because you can't swipe the card. Theoretically, the cost to acquire and keep the "terminal" should be minimal. However, when I signed up for a virtual terminal, the initial charge was only slightly less than the cost of purchasing a real terminal. But I did it anyway, because I also wanted to make sales from my web site.

Credit card companies charge several fees. There is a monthly charge, typically $5 to $50, for simply having the service. If you lease a terminal, that may be another $50 per month. There will be a discount applied to each transaction, probably somewhere in the range of 1.5% to 3% depending on sales volume. There will be a per-transaction charge, probably less than a dollar, and an authorization charge, also probably less than a dollar. All of these fees move significantly within their ranges depending upon a number of factors:

- Is the credit card in your hand and do you see the customer sign the voucher (as opposed to telephone or mail sales)?

- Is the card is swiped through a terminal so the magnetic information can be compared with the numbers on the front of the card?

- What resources are used at the credit card processor's end to authorize the transaction? Is it a telephone voice response system, a human operator, or a terminal to host electronic transaction?

- How many transactions are expected per month?

- What is the average dollar amount of each transaction?

- What type of credit card is it? (You may pay a full percentage point more in discounts for American Express than for Visa or MasterCard).

As a general rule, transactions authorized through a terminal are less expensive, but then there's the monthly cost of having the terminal. Consider a merchant service that will provide you with a "virtual terminal" so that you can obtain authorizations over the Internet using an onscreen menu to enter information. This will usually be cheaper than phone-in authorization because it requires fewer resources for the service, but the per-transaction fees will be a little higher because you have not scanned the card's magnetic stripe, which assures the service that you do not have a counterfeit card. But, you can also buy a magnetic stripe reader that attaches to your computer. Despite this advice, I have found that some credit card companies are charging up to $1,000 for a software package to make your computer act like a terminal. I do not see how that price is justified.

Talk to a number of merchant services, get rate sheets from each, and make sure you understand how the choices you make change the pricing structure. Then make a few assumptions about the number, dollar amount, and nature of credit card transactions you may expect in a month, and run the numbers on several scenarios per service. Consider these types of transactions in your mix:

What type and volume of transactions are likely to occur in your office (such as one divorce retainer per month at $3,000)?

Are you likely to have any telephone sales? Although I only practice in a couple of counties in Texas, I often receive telephone calls from people living out of state who must respond to a lawsuit in my county. It is impractical to ask them to fly down just for a consultation, and I see no reason to make exception to my rule of no free consultations, so it's convenient to offer them a telephone consultation paid for with a credit card.

Will you need to authorize any credit card transactions when you are away from your office, your terminal, and your computer? In the first few years of my practice I would accept "jail calls:" going to the jail in the middle of the night to run a writ of habeas corpus to force a bond to be set and then posting bond. Sometimes the family member meeting me at the jail needed to pay with a credit card – where I was away from my terminal, but I did have access to a telephone. If you expect a lot of this, you can get a terminal that uses cellular telephone technology to authorize charges – so you can process a credit card from the jail's waiting room, etc.

When looking for a merchant service, talk to your bank, several other banks in town, and several Internet-based companies. For the latest information on this quickly-changing industry, set your browser to your favorite search engine and ask it to search for "credit card merchant service" (without the quotes).

Photocopier

You'll want ready access to a copier that has a document feeder and a collator. You don't need a super fast copier, but you want something that can make five copies of a 40-page document without you tending it. In the copy room you'll want a heavy-duty stapler that can handle those thick documents.

There are also "digital copiers" which put a scanner in the same box as a heavy-duty laser printer. I cover this in more detail in the next chapter.

Facsimile

Despite the available alternative services, such as faxes as email attachments, you will want to have a fax machine, even if you only use it for sending faxes of documents in your file that you can't send directly from your computer. You may or may not want it to be part of a multi-function device (that's also a scanner and a printer, for instance). I advise spending the extra money for a plain paper model (instead of the rolls of thermal paper in earlier machines) because the thermal paper is very expensive, is difficult to handle and copy, and it fades with time. Having decided to use plain paper, it's your decision whether to use inkjet technology or a laser printer. Inkjet printers are cheaper to purchase, but cost more per printed page. If you anticipate receiving a comparatively small volume of faxes, go with inkjet.

.pdf: a fax alternative

This section doesn't really fit in the section on office equipment, but it's related to faxes, so I'll put it here. Anybody who uses technology much really dislikes faxes.

Lawyers often want to produce a document and have others review it without giving the reviewers the opportunity to simply change it. That is, you do not want to simply send a word processor file and have them change it, as you want to approve every single change. Faxes work well for this, but they take a long time to transmit, partly because fax transmission rates are a fraction of data transmission rates available over the Internet. Also, faxes of faxes degrade quickly into illegibility. But Adobe Acrobat is a software package that produces an image that cannot be edited on the other end, but can be printed as cleanly on the receiving end as it can on the sending end. The .pdf file produced by Acrobat can be attached to an email and sent in a fraction of the time for a fax. But, this only works if the receiving person has email. And while the Acrobat Reader (the software to read a .pdf file) can be downloaded for no charge from Adobe's web site (www.adobe.com), the "writer" software must be purchased, and it is not cheap.

I found it a worthwhile investment to purchase the Adobe Acrobat Writer software, although I use it far more in communication with my clients than I do with other lawyers, who are mostly stuck in fax technology. This may change as more counties go to electronic filing.

Printers

You'll need a computer and a laser printer. Inkjet printers are inexpensive and produce very attractive output, but the inkjet cartridges make the total cost of each page printed comparatively high, and they tend to print much more slowly than laser printers. The cost per page was prohibitively high until recently when inkjet manufacturers offered the ability to replace just the black ink cartridge instead of all of the colors.

Inkjet-printed pages may smear, especially if exposed to water. But inkjet printers also avoid many of the degrading quality problems experienced on inexpensive laser printers. You may be very satisfied with an inkjet printer if you don't print more than about a hundred pages a day.

There's a temptation to buy a big, fast, expensive laser printer and share it with others in the office. My advice is contrary to that. I think you should have a printer within arm's reach of where you normally work. The time and effort saved from not having to get up and go to the printer more than offsets the slightly longer printing time. And, to save a trip to the photocopier, I'll often just have my printer produce several copies of a short document (even if it costs a penny a page more to produce originals than to use the copier across the office).

I actually have four printers within arm's reach. First, I've got the laser printer, the workhorse, that cost less than $200 and prints 17 pages per minute. Then, I've got an inexpensive inkjet printer, that I keep loaded with envelopes, because my inkjet will feed from a stack of envelopes and my laser printer won't. Finally, I've got two dedicated label printers, for printing mailing labels and shipping labels.

Finally, here's a tip from the late Jim Seymour, a columnist with PC Magazine. If it's a hassle to print an envelope, print 3 and stick the other 2 in the file for future use.

Chapter 12
Computer Hardware

Lawyers are not computer power users. Computers are a huge benefit to lawyers, but lawyers do not need the fastest, most powerful computers. Lawyers tend to be slow to adopt new technology and slow to upgrade their systems. Long after the rest of the world had upgraded to Windows, many law offices were still happily working in DOS.

A lawyer's time is valuable, and nearly any investment in technology that results in greater productivity (less wasted time) for the lawyer will have a quick payback. But the applications at the heart of a law practice are document assembly and word processing, which will run quickly enough on comparatively modest equipment. But, lawyers are also cheap, and are slow to make their staff more efficient with new technology.

As a general rule, the most cost-effective way for a lawyer to buy computer equipment is to buy technology six months behind the leading edge. If the press is full of talk about the new WizBang VI processor and how fast it is, you should feel comfortable walking into a store and buying a WizBang V, knowing it's good enough, proven to be reliable, and has a much better return on investment.

Not only is the latest technology more expensive, but it's also more of a hassle. It may not have all the bugs worked out, and it may be a real chore finding other components or software that has been updated to be compatible with the new technology.

You may be tempted to overdo the advice to buy technology slightly older than the latest and greatest. You may be tempted to buy clearance bin technology. I advise against it. The latest and greatest processor may cost $300 installed in a computer, and one step back may cost half that. But going back a step farther may drop the price by less than twenty percent. Technology that is old enough to be significantly less expensive will either be inherently problematic or so old that it is difficult to find compatible software, drivers, peripherals, and so on.

It's very important that you develop or find expertise in computers. If you enjoy reading computer magazines, then you will probably be your own computer guru. If not, you'll want to develop a personal relationship with someone that owns a computer shop (not an employee). If you develop a relationship with a salesman, you may not be able to find them the next time you have a question. Talk to several gurus until you find someone that will try to save you money by steering you away from the very latest technology.

Americans tend to be very brand conscious. They think that a brand they recognize on their computer will buy them something. I have found that computers assembled by the no-name computer shop on the corner can be less expensive and just as reliable as a name-brand computer. Indeed, if something does go wrong and your blood pressure rises, you can walk into the local store with your computer in your arms and yell at somebody. Compare that to calling a long distance number, yelling at somebody who has no real power to help, and then waiting for UPS to come pick up your computer to fix it. Just make sure that your local computer shop has been around for several years and has few complaints from the Better Business Bureau.

As much as I hate to, I suppose I'll have to weigh in on the PC vs. Mac issue. Actually, the issue has broadened lately, with some additional operating systems becoming available.

I *like* Macs. I *like* additional operating system choices (I have an Amiga computer in the garage that's a marvel). I like that some of the new operating systems, mostly UNIX-based, are much more reliable than Windows. But before you venture away from the herd, realize you dramatically decrease your choices in everything you do with your computer. There are probably hundreds of word processing packages that will run under Windows, but only a handful that will run under the Mac OS, and maybe only one or two that run under Linux. You may or may not be able to find CD-ROM legal research materials that will work in your non-Windows environment. Document assembly software likewise may not be available. Most of all, you will have far fewer experts available to help you with system problems, and you will have to be your own expert. If your computer is your hobby instead of your tool, you're probably taking most of my advice in this chapter with a large grain of salt, and you should do what you want to do. For everybody else, I recommend you stay with the Windows operating system.

Equipping your computer

Do not cut corners by putting too little RAM (memory) in your computer. An extra $200 spent here at the time of purchase can save you hours of waiting time over the course of a year. And do not be afraid to upgrade the RAM in a year or two.

Although you do not need a hard disk drive (storage) that is so large that it is on the cutting edge, you do want a reasonably large hard drive. However big it is, you'll need to upgrade to a bigger one in a couple of years. But, they don't make them now as big as you'll need in a couple of years, and it'll only cost a hundred dollars to upgrade it then.

You'll also need three forms of removable storage. You'll need a 3½-inch floppy disk drive and a CD-ROM drive because that is how most software is delivered (despite inroads in online software delivery over the Internet).

The third removable storage device you'll need is a backup tape drive. Or, get a CD "burner" instead of just a CD reader. Or even a DVD burner. I'll cover backup procedures in more detail in a later chapter, but this much needs to be said now. The most convenient way to back up is to start a backup when you leave the office and to find it done when you return. If your backup medium is not big enough to hold everything on the hard disk, you'll return to the office, switch media, and wait some more. Then you'll swap again (twice) while it verifies the backup. I have experimented with backup media other than tape and do not recommend them. I have found them delicate, unreliable, too small to hold everything, and not fast enough to be a practical alternative to tape.

Burning CD-ROMs is attractive, but it still requires considerable human intervention in the form of disk-swapping to do a complete backup. If a DVD-burner is cost-effective, then it may be a good alternative, because you can do a complete backup while you're away from the office (and unavailable to swap disks).

Allow me a brief diversion on floppy disks, please. Back when personal computers were new and there were such things as standalone word processors, the floppy disk was invented. Think of an 8-inch or 5¼-inch diameter platter of flexible mylar, enclosed in an envelope of shirtboard with slots cut out for the machine to have access to the medium. The entire package could easily be bent between thumb and fingers. Later, the 3½-inch disk was developed, with a rigid plastic shell enclosing the medium and a door that the machine opened to access the medium. Because the new storage medium felt rigid to the hand, some people called these hard disks to differentiate them from the floppy ones that had come before. But the reason the earlier ones had been called floppy was because the medium itself was floppy, instead of bonded to something rigid, such as aluminum. So, the newer hard-cased disks were still properly called floppy disks because the medium inside remained floppy.

There have continued to be developments in floppy disks, notably the Zip drive, which have capacities in the hundreds of megabytes (a 3½-inch floppy has a capacity of 1.44 megabytes). High-capacity floppy drives have caught on in the graphics industry, where very large files must be transported from artist to service bureau, but have not caught on anywhere else. Large software packages are now delivered on CD-ROM, which is very inexpensive to reproduce, and offers several times the storage of a super floppy.

Another development is the removable hard disk. Among the first in this category was the Bernoulli Box, and recent entries have been the Jaz and the Sparq. The newer entries do not look remarkably different on the outside from a super floppy. Again, what makes these "hard" disks is that the medium inside the container is rigid (with a metal core). These can be spun much faster inside the drive and this increases data transfer rates. Data can be written more compactly, so storage capacity is greater. They are also more expensive to produce, so the price per disk is several times as much as a super floppy. I have experimented with these as backup media and have found them unreliable and too small to back up all of my hard drive.

Another mass-storage avenue you may wish to pursue is optical storage. Floppy disks and hard disks are both magnetic media, but CD-ROMs are optical. A laser is pointed at the CD and the reflections are read to determine what was written to the CD. You must have a CD-ROM drive on your system for installing software and for large databases, such as from legal research services. DVD (Digital Video Disk) is a variant, and most DVD drives will also read CD-ROMs, with the advantage of much greater storage capacity, and the ability to watch movies on your computer (not something that interests me). But you can also buy a CD-R, or a CD "burner," which allows you to record CDs. Although CDs do not have the capacity of a large backup tape, they are quite inexpensive and reliable. You can even use one to make audio CDs that you can play at home or in the car.

I know a few lawyers that will only keep active files on their computer. When they close a case, they will transfer all files relating to that case to a floppy disk, put the floppy in the paper file, and archive it. I do not recommend this practice. First, it takes too much time. Second, floppy disks are more "forgetful" than hard drives, so you run a higher chance of losing your data. Third, hard drives are cheap and upgrading every couple of years for a couple of hundred dollars will give you the additional capacity of thousands of floppy disks. Fourth, if it's on the hard drive, you can back it up to tape. Fifth, if it's on your hard drive you can find it with indexing software even if you don't remember the client's name (see the chapter on utilities).

Monitor

Invest in a larger monitor. A 17-inch monitor would be the minimum, and if you want to do yourself a favor, get a 19-inch. Indeed, if I had a choice between a color 17-inch monitor and a good monochrome (black and white) 19-inch monitor, I'd take the 19-inch. I've got a 19-inch color monitor I spent a couple of hundred dollars on, and it's great. The more real estate you have for displaying data, the more things you can have on screen at once. This will save considerable time by simply glancing at the information you need instead of having to bring the right program to the front and finding the information. This is one of the main justifications for the Windows operating system (as compared to DOS, which it replaced), but most users just have one application on screen at a time. A much larger monitor can help you achieve the full potential of the operating system.

Flat-screen monitors are just becoming affordable as I write this. If you can afford a flat screen and want one, go ahead. But, I urge you not to buy a smaller monitor just to get a flat screen. I'd rather have a big, bulky CRT 19-inch display than a trim, flat 17-inch display, simply because the extra real estate is so valuable. Also, as of this writing, CRT monitors are clearer and sharper than flat panels. So, if you can live with the depth of a CRT monitor, it'll cost you less and give you more information on screen.

UPS

Consider an Uninterruptible Power Supply ("UPS" or battery backup). A small one will cost less than $100 and will allow you to save your work if the power fails. More important is that a UPS can also make your computer immune to short power interruptions and brownouts.

Laptop computers

Laptop computers can be very useful to the lawyer. Your office is anywhere you find yourself with your computer. Sometimes if you couldn't take your office with you on vacation you wouldn't be able to go on vacation at all. I have found it particularly useful to bring a laptop computer with document assembly software on it to mediations so that we can leave with a signed order instead of simply a memorandum of settlement (which leaves countless details to be negotiated over the coming weeks).

One can be tempted to make a laptop computer the only computer for the office. My former advice was not to do it. But for a couple of years Ie worked on a laptop connected to a local network. Backing up files from a laptop is usually a hassle, but in this case I just sent the files over the network to the server, and back the server up. If you decide to use a laptop as your primary computer, spend the extra money to attach a real keyboard and a real mouse (or trackball) to it, and consider hooking up a bigger monitor.

Digital copiers

Digital copiers are an interesting twist. The idea is to combine a very fast laser printer with a photocopier. The technological challenge is that while photocopiers and laser printers both put an image on a drum, pick up toner, and transfer the toner to paper, one is done using a positive electrical charge and the other is done with a negative charge. So, simply dropping a laser into a photocopier won't do the job. The response is to combine a laser printer with a scanner, but arrange the whole apparatus so that it looks like a photocopier.

When you step up to a digital copier to make a copy, you don't really make a copy in the usual sense. The computer inside the copier tells the scanner to scan the document, then tells the printer to print so many copies. Although it's technologically different, the person making the copies can't tell the difference.

The same machine can also be a networked printer for all the computers in the office, making copies much faster than they could be made on a small printer beside the computer. Instead of making an original and then making copies, you simply print as many originals as you need. Things get a little more complicated when you want copies that have your signature on them: you can sign several originals, you can stamp the copies "original signed by …", you can use a digital image of your signature, or you can sign the signature page and then copy it.

The scanner on a digital copier is also fast and networked, so it's easy to scan documents to archive them or email them to clients.

While a digital copier offers many advantages to a law office with networked computers (a law firm, or at least a lawyer and a secretary), I am not fully sold on them for the solo lawyer. For the copier part of the machine to work as you need it, it must be fairly fast, it must have a document feeder and some sort of collating ability. Aside from raising the price, this also increases the size of the machine, making it too large to place with the output within arm's reach of the chair where you'll be working on the computer. If you must stand up, walk around the desk, maybe out of the office and down the hall to pick up a one-page letter and three copies, you have lost a lot of efficiency. My little, inexpensive desktop laser prints 17 pages per minute, and for any job less than about 12 pages I'll just print multiple originals. Also try to figure out how you'll print envelopes and mailing labels using a digital copier.

Finally, I have not yet seen digital copiers that are affordable and have an output sorter, like you'll see on most law office photocopiers. I believe that a copier without an output sorter is too inefficient to use.

When you first open your office, you'll probably be borrowing someone else's copier, or you'll buy a used or refurbished copier. Only when the prices of digital copiers approach those of regular copiers should you consider purchasing one, unless your office grows to the point that you have installed a network and could benefit from a large, fast printer that also serves as a copier. Even then, consider keeping your desktop printer for convenience on smaller jobs and for printing envelopes.

Networking

Since the first edition of this book was published, I have set up an office network. That may seem strange for a solo lawyer, but recently I've had some part-time help, and another computer became a necessity. As the cost of desktop computers plummet, it becomes more and more attractive to form a network. I like the fact that my old laptop computer has instant access to a very large hard drive that is backed up regularly. It's also nice that my son can do his homework at the office where we share a high-speed internet connection over the network.

I've found that it's fairly easy to set up a basic peer-to-peer network if all the computers use the same (recent) operating system. This has surprised me, as I had always believed that being a network administrator in a small office was a sentence to hell.

Chapter 13
Very Portable Computing

I am an advocate for handheld computers, but even if you are convinced you do not want or need a handheld computer you should read this chapter. This is where I write about the core organizational functions of address book, calendar, to-do list, and billable time. You need to understand how critical these functions are to the profitability of your practice, and how essential they are in avoiding grievances and malpractice claims, even if you use pen and paper to accomplish them.

When starting your practice, you will find it easier to get clients for litigation work, which will necessarily take you out of your office a large percentage of the time. Even if you are experienced in transactional work and do nothing but that, you should be spending a fair amount of time out of the office trying to meet your next client. Any time you are out of the office, you simply must have your calendar and address book with you so that you can make an appointment with the client you just lined up, pass on a useful contact, or enter a "to-do" item to follow up on something.

Paper calendars are too large to just drop in your pocket. And if you ever lose a paper calendar, you are absolutely sunk, because there is no backup. With a pocket computer you can have your calendar, phone book, and to-do list with you at all times. And if your handheld is lost, destroyed, or stolen, all it takes is money to put you back in commission. You can buy a new handheld at the office supply, drop it in the cradle in your office, and synchronize, and the only information you have lost is the information you put in since you last synchronized.

Before pocket computers, I would use a desktop Personal Information Manager ("PIM") to track all of my contacts and calendar. Each day when I left the office I would print out a piece of paper with the current to-do items, a detail of the day's schedule, and a summary of the next month. Then I'd print another few pages with the summary for the next few months. This was useful for keeping track of my schedule: in court I could announce whether or not I had a conflict on a certain day. Then I'd write any changes on the paper, and when I got back to the office I'd update my computer. This system worked fairly well except for two problems. First, I did not have current addresses and telephone numbers for my clients at hand, so if something came unglued at the courthouse I'd be unable to contact my afternoon appointment to let them know I needed to reschedule. Second, writing schedule information on my paper and then reentering it on my office computer meant double work.

My first experiment with portable computing was a Hewlett Packard 200LX. This was too large and bulky to be conveniently carried in a pocket, but I did so anyway. Synchronization was rudimentary: I had to keep track of which computer was current, and when I got back to the office I'd simply use the data in the portable computer to replace the data in the desktop computer. Although large and inelegant, it worked remarkably well.

Beginning with the Pilot (which is what the first two versions of what we now call Palm were called) synchronization finally worked: the operating system kept track of which records were new or changed on each computer, and automatically updated the other computer properly.

I have experimented with Windows CE portable computers, but have found them slow and clumsy compared to the ones using the Palm OS. Although they may have several times as much memory as a Palm, I found that they needed several times as much memory to get the job done. The menu system was cumbersome, and entering a time other than on the hour, such as 3:10 p.m., took much longer to enter than on a Palm. As of this writing, handheld computers using the Palm Operating System ("Palm OS") had a huge market share, over 80%, so I will focus on Palm handheld computers. Most of the underlying principles can be applied to other handheld computers. See www.palm.com and www.handspring.com.

There are a large number of desktop PIMs, alternatively called Contact Managers, most of them much more capable than the Palm Desktop, which comes with the Palm handheld computers. For example, the Palm Desktop will not keep track of titles that go in front of or behind a person's name, such as "Mr." or "Jr.," will not track a real name and a nick name, and does not have a field for a second (home) address. These are all functions that most other desktop PIMs have. On the other hand, the simplicity of the Palm Desktop is a blessing, because there are only three basic screens per contact, instead of ten or more with some systems.

Some of these other PIMs have customized versions of the HotSync Manager to allow them to synchronize with the Palm. But I have found that there is always some quirk in the synchronization that causes me to lose data, so I always go back to the Palm Desktop. These problems with other PIMs usually revolve around the Note field in the Palm, which I use as a repository for any other information I may need about the person that doesn't fit in another field. For friends, it may be a home address. For clients, it may be the name and contact information for opposing counsel, and I may put driving directions to my client's house if I have ever needed to hand deliver documents. For vendors or other attorneys, I may put in some key words for what they do so that I can recall them using the "Find" feature.

One extremely capable PIM is ACT! (which is actually more of a contact manager than a PIM, but the differences are mostly academic for our purposes) (www.actsoftware.com). ACT! doesn't have a Note field in the same sense that Palm does: ACT! uses Notes (plural) to keep track of previous contacts with the person, such as telephone calls or letters. I found to my horror that the wonderful information I had stored in "Note" in my Palm (such as the client's home address) was being deleted to make room for information about my latest telephone call.

PIMs and contact managers can also be too smart for my own good. Some will interpret a comma in the name as having entered the last name before the first name, and will reorder the information for you. I have found "William Smith, Jr." filed under "W" (apparently "Jr." was taken as a first name). Some PIMs will not accept the fact that sometimes you just don't care to whom you talk at a company: you leave the field for the last name blank and the software doesn't know what to do: they are people-based, so "Lotus Technical Support" must be a person whose last name is Support.

Finally, no matter how good the desktop application is, having more detailed information on your desktop doesn't do you any good when you are out of the office and have to rely on your handheld. That's another reason I have chosen to find ways to make the software that comes with my handheld work rather than switching to a more capable desktop application.

Core applications

Whatever desktop application you use, and whether you use a Palm, a Windows CE device, or paper printouts from your desktop application, the core applications they all use are the ones that can keep you out of trouble in the practice of law if you use them properly. Here are the core applications:

Calendar

Phone Book

To-do List

Memo

Calendar

Calendar is where you keep track of all of your appointments. It's not a tricky application, but it can make the difference between client satisfaction and a malpractice suit. Obviously, you should use this to track all of your appointments. But take care to enter enough information about each appointment.

One of the first persons to attend my seminar, let's call him Jim, had been practicing law for several months, and had been doing a great job of getting clients. But he had absolutely no organization. He had a paper calendar book, but if a new prospective client booked an appointment, the lawyer would only write down the person's name in the proper place in his calendar. If Jim got hung up in court he only had enough information to cause anxiety and not enough to find relief. There was no phone number to call to tell the prospective client that the meeting would have to be rescheduled.

I make a new Phone Book entry for every person who contacts me about legal services. If they don't hire me, I use the information to follow-up with phone calls and letters. If they don't hire me after a year, I purge them.

I believe the minimum information needed in your calendar for the first consultation with a prospective client are: who, what, when, where, referral source, and telephone number. "Who" is the name of the person. "What" is the subject matter, so you'll know what forms to hand them when they show up. The "when" will be covered by where you put it in the calendar, and "where" will be assumed to be in your office unless you put something else down. You'll need a telephone number to call if something goes awry and you need to reschedule the appointment.

"Referral source" is absolutely critical to the growth of your practice. If it was an advertisement, you'll want to know which advertising is paying for itself. If the client was referred by a former client, you'll need to send a thank-you note. If the referral came from another lawyer, you'll need to send a thank-you note and maybe a check for a referral fee. Periodically you'll need to review your appointments and see which sources are working best for you and figure out who you need to take to lunch or a ball game.

While you really don't have to have the referral source information at the time you book the appointment, I have found that the longer the time between the first telephone call and the actual consultation, the fuzzier the memory is of how they got your name. My recommendation is to ask the prospect where they got your name at the time you make the appointment.

Here's an example of a client consultation calendar entry: "Bill Jones re div fr Dallas LRS w972-555-1234 m972-555-5678." Interpretation: Bill Jones regarding a divorce, he got my name from the Dallas Lawyer Referral Service, his work phone number is 972-555-1234 and his mobile number is 972-555-5678.

For appointments other than initial consultations, such as court appearances, I still like to put plenty of information down. If it's a court appearance, I will at least put down the nature of the court appearance, the name of the client, and the name of the court. "Crutchfield 1st app 366th" tells me that my client, Ms. Crutchfield, has her first appearance on a criminal matter in the 366th District Court on that date. With a glance at my calendar I'll know which courtroom to go to. Also, if Ms. Crutchfield calls me and asks when our next court date is, I can use the "Find" feature to find her name, and the court dates will pop right up.

Phone book

Jim, the same fellow I wrote about in the previous section, had another organizational problem. When he signed up a new client, he did not use a client intake form and did not have a telephone book. In the course of the initial interview, it would sometimes occur to him to ask the person their telephone number, which would be written in the margin of the legal pad on which he was taking his notes. The only way he could call his client is if he found the paper client file first. This was often impractical if he was at the courthouse (on another matter) and the file was in the office.

The majority of malpractice insurance claims and grievances with the bar associations are essentially failure to communicate with the client. Clients will forgive nearly anything if you communicate with them quickly and often, 'fess up to your failings, and make a sincere effort to make things better. Even if you are doing a great job, the client will assume the worst if he or she does not hear from you.

No news is assumed to be bad news. It is not enough to do the work the client needs done: you must also make sure that the client knows that you are working on the case. Every time you do something on the case, find an opportunity to produce a writing, such as a draft document or a confirming letter with opposing counsel, even if it's a two-sentence letter or email ("This happened. Call if you have a question"). There should be a confirming letter after nearly any communication with the courts or opposing counsel. Always print two extra copies: one for your file and one for the client. You don't need a cover letter for your client, just a rubber stamp that says, "Client Copy: Please Retain for Your Records." Stamp a copy, stuff it in an envelope, and send it to the client. Additional time and effort on your part is nearly nothing, and the client knows you did something. Part of your mission in life is to make the client's file at his home as thick as the one in your office.

You won't write lots of confirming letters or send copies to your client if it takes a lot of time and effort to create and address a letter. A good phone book makes this easy.

Any decent phone book, including the one in the Palm Desktop, provides a convenient way of addressing a letter. Usually you'll just call up the person's record, click on an icon, and the person's address will be copied to Windows' clipboard. You just go to your word processor and ctrl-v paste the address into the letter.

Because most of my clients are individuals rather than companies, I do not usually need the name of the company or the person's title with the company. I use those fields in my phone book for other information. In the "title" field I will put my file number for the client (see the chapter on organizing your paper files). That way, even if the case is closed, I can find the file quickly in storage. In the "company" field I will put the "subject" information I want to appear in the letter, such as, "In the Matter of the Marriage of John R. Doe and Suzie Q. Doe, and in the Interest of Children, No. 219-12345-03." The last number is the docket number assigned by the court clerk.

Palm's phone book has four user-defined fields. I have renamed one "source" and another "practice area." I'll use the first to track how that person found out about me for marketing analysis. I'll use the second for analysis on the practice areas that are growing and shrinking.

I like to put the contact information for opposing counsel in the Note field of my client's record. If I need to write a letter to opposing counsel, even when I don't remember opposing counsel's name, I just drag my client's record to the clipboard. My letter has my client's name and address, the subject, and opposing counsel's name and address all right there. I've even got fax numbers for me to copy into WinFax if I need to fax the letter directly from my computer. Cutting and pasting information such as fax numbers eliminates opportunities for transcription errors, and is faster as well.

To-do

Every malpractice insurance application I have seen contains several questions about ticklers. Ticklers are simply ways of reminding yourself of something on a certain date. Lawyers do not use tickler systems often enough, and too many lawyers get sued when the lawyer forgets to file a lawsuit before the statute of limitations passes. It's easy to do: you're in the middle of negotiations and the other side is being reasonably responsive, so you hope to settle before the lawsuit is filed. But you will be distracted by other cases, or by the minutiæ of the same case, and once the deadline for filing is passed, the other side is no longer interested in negotiating.

Many folks use the to-do list just for things they plan to do when they get to the office the next day. While that's an excellent use of the to-do list, it doesn't exploit the full potential. When you add an item to the to-do list, you can also set a due date as some time in the future. With Palm's preferences set to show only items that are due, that item will not show up on your to-do list until the due date you have set. Example: in Texas, a petition for divorce must be on file for at least 60 days before the divorce can be granted. When I sign up a client for a divorce that looks like it could be a minimum-time agreed divorce, I'll add a to-do item 55 days or so in the future, such as, "Jones 60d up 4/17." If things are still contested when it pops up on my to-do list, I'll just check it off. If the case is ready, I'll call the client and arrange a mutually convenient date to prove up the divorce.

Anyone who tries to negotiate a settlement before filing a lawsuit, especially consumer or injury cases, should add a reminder a month or so before the limitations period lapses in each case. Similarly, discovery deadlines should show up in the to-do list a few days before the actual deadline.

Memo

I find the Memo application in the Palm is very useful, but few of my attorney friends use it. It is amazing what can be stored and kept at hand. Here are some of the frivolous and mundane things in my Memo application:

- My son's class schedule

- The script for "Make Sure He Doesn't Leave" from Monty Python's *Holy Grail.*

- My blood pressure log

- What my family members want for Christmas

- The lyrics and chords for the song, "Poor Wayfaring Stranger"

- My recipe for Sweet Potato Custard Pie

- A collection of Yogi Berra wit

- The complete text of the poem "The Face on the Barroom Floor" by Hugh Antoine

There are three important things I keep in my "Business" category of Memo. First is an outline of an area of the law I often need to know on the spur of the moment. I used to be a part-time municipal judge, and it was my duty to arraign prisoners at the jail. There are complex rules involving minors, alcohol, tobacco, driver's license suspension, community service, and special classes. Plus, the rules change every two years when the legislature meets. If I had an 18-

year-old in front of me who was arrested on a warrant arising from incident two years ago, I'll need to know whether he was a "juvenile" at the time of the offense according to the code then, whether he has to take a special class, what happens if he doesn't, and how much community service I have to order. Memo is perfect for keeping this sort of thing available on a moment's notice.

The second important business item I keep in Memo is the script for helping a client plead guilty. I have never been any good at memorizing things, and without a script all I can remember is, "Comes now the defendant and admits that his true name is John Philip Sousa. He waives arraignment and he waives reading of the indictment. He knows and understands he has the right to [something about a jury] and he waives that right. He knows and understands he has the right to [something about making the State bring witnesses to testify so he can cross examine them, and something about subpoenaing his own witnesses] and he gives up that right [shouldn't it be *those* rights?]. [Blah, blah, something about the State having permission to use his stipulation of facts, and on and on]. With the script in my Palm Pilot Memo, I'm always prepared. Think about what information you need to have at your fingertips, or wish you could memorize.

Before I go on to the last important business area for Memo, let me point something out. Entering all of these interesting facts into a handheld computer using handwriting recognition (Graffiti) would be *very* tedious. Much of what I have in Memo would not be there if I had to enter it by hand. The best way to get more than a few lines of information into your handheld computer is to type it or paste it into your desktop computer and then synchronize your handheld.

I can go into Palm Desktop's Memo application and type whatever I need into a new record. With a push of the Synchronize button, that data appears in my handheld. Moving information from a word processing document or from the Internet is even easier. While viewing the information in Windows, I highlight what I want, type control-c to copy it to the clipboard, put my cursor in the desktop memo, and type control-v to paste it in. I synchronize and I'm done.

Time and billing

The most important use for Memo for me is keeping track of billable time so I can get paid for it. The most widely used time and billing software is Timeslips, but it's mostly useful for folks who sit in their office all day long. For those of us who are often billing time out of the office, it is very useful to keep track of time in Memo. I have tried a palmtop version of Timeslips, but found it too complex, as I don't do much work that's paid by the hour.

The key to making Memo useful for tracking billable time is using Shortcuts, which are set up in system preferences. The Palm comes with a number of predefined shortcuts, and you may define more. When in any application on the Palm handheld, you may draw a lower case script L and then another character or two and the system will automatically drop in the phrase you have defined. For example, dts (date and time stamp) will drop in the current date and the current time.

Here are the shortcuts on my handheld:

- ds [date stamp]

- dts [date and time stamp]

- hr attend hearing

- lm left message

- me meeting with client in office;

- oc opposing counsel

- tc telephone call with client;

- ts [time stamp]

These are best used in combination. If my opposing counsel calls me when I am out of the office and my phone is forwarded to my mobile phone, at the conclusion of the telephone call I'll open my client's Memo and type /dts, then /tc, then I'll erase the word "client" and type /oc, then I'll type 0.2. The result is "07/02/00 10:03 a.m. telephone call with opposing counsel; 0.2"

As a general rule I will separate the different activities during a day with semicolons and create a new paragraph with a date stamp each day. Note that some of my shortcuts end in a semicolon. During the day, when I add an item, I will update the total time at the end of the paragraph, rather than keeping time for each individual item.

I could have a lot more shortcuts, such as for logging emails received or sent, letters drafted, letters from counsel reviewed, etc., but these are activities that normally happen at the office, and I can note these with a full-sized keyboard instead of trying to use Graffiti to get them logged.

When I'm ready to send my client a bill, I'll start a letter in my word processor, with standard boilerplate language as "this is to bill you for my time on your case since my last bill." Then I'll just cut and paste the information from the Memo into my word processor. I've got a very simple spreadsheet programmed into my standard billing letter which takes care of the arithmetic in comparing billed time to the amount on retainer, money received during the period, out of pocket expenditures during the period, target retainer, and "please remit."

I find this system simple, direct, and less hassle than using another software package.

A few years ago I switched to the Handspring Treo for my pocket device, because it was also a phone, and had internet capability. It was a relief to get away from carrying around a phone and a pocket computer. However, the device proved quite fragile and unreliable (I sent it back to the factory 6 times in 18 months), so I've gone back to having a separate phone and PDA.

Financial Calculator

The calculator that comes with the handheld is a simple four-function calculator with memory. That works fine for most purposes, but when I am working on a divorce I often need to calculate the present value of future child support payments to determine how much life insurance needs to in place, or to figure out the value of a retirement plan. Personal injury lawyers need to figure the value of a structured settlement. To do these types of calculations you really need a financial calculator.

Rather than carry my Hewlett Packard 12c Financial Calculator with me at all times, I found a software emulation of the same calculator that can be downloaded into my handheld. The one I happen to use is Abacus, which can be downloaded from www.dovcom.com. Warning: this calculator uses Reverse Polish Notation or RPN, for which Hewlett Packard calculators are either famous or infamous depending on your viewpoint. If you don't know how to work a calculator that doesn't have an equal key, look for another financial calculator that uses algebraic notation.

Email

I hate sounding like a Luddite, and I plan to revise this book before it gets out of date, but I do not believe that email-enabled handheld computers are very important to the solo lawyer, at least not yet.

The story is different for lawyers who have a legal assistant or secretary minding the store for them while the lawyer is at the courthouse (or golf course). It would be great to be sitting in the courtroom during a docket call and be able to send terse emails back to someone who ought to be working, like, "Is the Smithers lease ready to go out?" or "Please ask Johnson if she'd mind rescheduling our 1:00 meeting to 3:30."

The problems with email on the palmtop computer is that there is too little memory to store all of one's email, the display is too small to display a significant amount of a long email, attachments would be difficult or impossible to open, replies of more than a few words would be too tedious to enter with handwriting recognition, and it is expensive.

For the brand-new solo lawyer, it is too expensive, slow, and clumsy to do all of your email from a handheld computer, so care must be taken to only send short urgent messages to and from the handheld. I know I would just get messages like, "Please pick up the dry cleaning on your way home," and other messages that can just as easily be sent via voice mail, or by text messages to my mobile phone.

Having just dismissed handheld email, I recommend that you watch developments in this field, as it may become much more practical soon.

Chapter 14
Software

Nowhere else in this book is my advice more specific, nor more likely to become dated in a short period of time. I plan to update this book in general and this chapter in particular frequently. Fortunately, advances in printing technology have made it economically feasible to print shorter and shorter runs of books, so it is also more feasible to revise a book frequently.

For some applications, such as legal research or document assembly, you will have to use applications designed specifically for lawyers. But my philosophy is that when you don't have to use a lawyer-specific application, you are better off with applications designed for the average non-lawyer. For example, for years the most popular word processor for lawyers was Word Perfect (www.corel.com), but not because Word Perfect is any easier to use or has any better features that lawyers use. Word Perfect was the premiere word processor in the years before the Windows operating system became accepted around 1991. As lawyers were dragged, kicking and screaming, into the Windows operating system, they continued to use the word processor they were used to, although the rest of the world recognized at the time that Word Perfect for Windows was the third best word processor for Windows. Now while it is understandable that lawyers who knew how to use one program would resist learning a new one, it does not explain why so many lawyers without any particular word processing preference would start out learning the third-best program in its class. I believe the answer is that lawyers thought their needs were different from everybody else's, and found it easier to blindly follow the recommendations of other lawyers rather than research it themselves.

I also think that lawyers have rationalized their choice by saying that it would be easier to exchange documents and forms with one another if they used the same software as most other lawyers. My response is twofold. First, that may have been true in the past, but conversion routines in modern programs make it very easy to import files from other word processors into whatever word processor you choose. Second, I find myself trying to share documents with my clients far more often than with other lawyers, and the overwhelming choice of non-lawyers is strikingly different from that of lawyers.

Word processors

The word processor wars are over for the non-lawyer world, and the overwhelming winner is Microsoft's Word for Windows, or WinWord. I have been proficient in several different word processors since 1980, and I still do not feel fully comfortable in WinWord, but I believe it is because it will never be my "first" word processor. I am used to the command logic and structure of other word processors and I find WinWord counterintuitive (ah, how I long for WordStar and its menu structure you could memorize and operate with your hands constantly in their "native" positions on the keyboard). Nonetheless I have WinWord on my computer and I use it frequently, because it is the *lingua franca* of the business world. It certainly has every conceivable feature one could want in a word processor, and I recommend it without hesitation, especially to anyone who has not formed an association with another word processor.

WinWord is also part of Microsoft's Office package of applications, which are all designed to work together. This concept works well when you need to convert something you have already produced in one application into something that's quite different. If you have produced a draft brochure in WinWord, you can move the text over to Publisher to convert it into a word page or into a mailing piece. Although Microsoft Office is an expensive suite of programs, the applications do work together and each application is at least pretty good (no worse than the second-best application in its field, while several are the best available).

WinWord will easily handle forms created in other word processors, such as Word Perfect. My document assembly (forms) software naturally produces documents in Word Perfect format and then converts them to WinWord format, and this works reasonably well.

Document Assembly

Lawyers may not have invented the phrase, "reduce, reuse, recycle," but lawyers have been recycling legal verbiage since before the term recycling came into being. From the time you open your practice until the day you die, legal publishers' salesmen will be calling you, trying to sell you legal resource books and forms.

Formbooks on paper are an interesting way to study the law, but they are very inefficient for producing the pleading you need. While paper formbooks are available, they are not useful to the solo lawyer unless they are accompanied by forms on disk. It doesn't make sense to type every document from scratch.

Expect to pay for formbooks on a monthly basis. You're not just paying for the book, you're paying to have it updated whenever the law changes. You should receive updates periodically.

To select formbooks, visit the continuing legal education seminars in your fields of expertise. Talk to the vendors who have tables outside the meeting room, and during breaks ask your fellow attendees what they like to use and why. Preferences will change from practice area to practice area and from state to state, perhaps city to city.

Basic forms on disk are inexpensive but comparatively difficult to use. There is no intelligence to the system: there is simply a large word processing document that you manually customize as necessary.

The more expensive and more useful alternative is document assembly. Document assembly software gets inside the logic of the form and asks interactive questions of the user about how the document is to be structured. For example, if assembling a divorce decree, one of the first questions will be whether there are any children. If the answer is no, great huge sections of the basic form are bypassed because they are inapplicable, and you are not asked questions about children for the rest of the document.

Document assembly software will also track information from document to document for a given client. Once you have told the system your client's name and the cause number in the first pleading, the system should not ask you again for any other pleading for the same matter.

Because forms must be different for every jurisdiction and practice area, it is impossible for me to make a meaningful recommendation on specific software.

Legal Research

The oldest names in online legal research are Westlaw and Lexis. Each has its own peculiar logic for finding cases. Westlaw has its Keycite legal index numbering system that is marketed as true value-added intellectual property, and accordingly they typically charge more than the competition. A recent entry is LOIS, short for Law Office Information System, which provides legal research at a lower cost than the two front-runners. There is also FindLaw.com, and probably several more will be added before you read this.

If you are a recent law school graduate, you probably had free legal research accounts with one or more online legal research systems, and you have probably made up your mind regarding your preferences.

In my first year of law practice, I found that the cases I was getting were not fringe cases. The law was not really a matter of debate, but the application of the facts to the law was. I would find myself referring frequently to my annotated code books, but only about twice in my first year did I need to find a case or establish the authority of a case. Online legal research was over $100 per month, and an expense I just didn't need, so when I did have a matter come up I would go to the local law library, or go to a neighboring lawyer's office.

I urge you to keep a list taped to your computer monitor, or perhaps in a memo in your palmtop computing device, listing the date and nature of every time you wished you had online legal research capability, and exactly what task you would research. Then go ahead and borrow a friend's law library or online research system or go to the law library. Every time you make a new entry in your list, look at how many entries you have in the last six months. If you have a dozen entries in the last six months, then you should probably get online legal research capability in your office. But your list will also guide you in selecting a service, because you'll know how many were on federal law, how many were on state law, how many started with a statute, and how many were looking for a key phrase.

Lawyer's Trust Account

Many of the folks who attend my seminars do not understand how a lawyer's trust account is supposed to work, and trust account errors account for a significant number of attorney grievances filed each year. If you have been practicing law for several years, particularly with a firm, you may wish to skip this section.

There are a number of reasons why a lawyer will have control of money that does not belong to him. The lawyer may receive the proceeds of a settlement, and may need to settle various other claims before the net proceeds are distributed to the client (and to the lawyer if a contingent fee is involved). In a divorce, the other side may be concerned that your client will spend her bonus before the courts decide how it should be split, so opposing counsel may ask you to take the bonus into your trust account pending a court decision or a settlement agreement. Most commonly, a client may deposit money with you against your legal fees and expenses.

The lawyer is charged with taking care of the money entrusted to him and never converting any portion of it to personal use without following proper procedures. Remember all the cases from law school about the duties of a fiduciary.

The new lawyer will open two checking accounts. The first will be his operating account, into which he will place all the money he has earned, and from which he will pay all of the office bills and write a check for the remainder to put in his personal account.

The second account he will open is the lawyers trust account. I suggest you try to make the accounts as different as possible without putting them in separate banks. I use blue stock for my operating account checks, and green stock for trust account checks. My trust account checks started their numbers with 1000, and my operating account checks started at 3000. I use a large black-ink endorsement stamp for one account, and a small red-ink stamp for the other. I use wallet sized deposit slips for my operating account, and business sized deposit slips for my trust account. All this is to make sure you I never accidentally put money into the wrong account, or remove it from the wrong account.

Remember two principles about your trust account: never mingle your money with the client's money, and keep track of how much money you have that belongs to each client. If you disregard either of these principles, you'll likely lose your law license.

Let's suppose that I have two new clients sign up one day. Client Adams wants a will, and Client Baker needs a divorce. For Client Adams, I quote a fixed fee after our initial consultation, and he signs a letter of agreement agreeing to the flat fee. I will deposit that money directly into my operating account, because that entire fee has been earned (when I deposited the check the money already belonged solely to me).

Client Baker signs a letter of agreement with me agreeing that I will be paid at $280 per hour, that there will be a minimum fee of $1900, and that she has deposited $5,000 with me toward my fees and costs. The $5,000 is referred to as a retainer, or more precisely as a combination retainer and cost deposit. A retainer is not a minimum fee: it is simply an amount placed on deposit to guarantee payment of future fees. (By the way, I strongly discourage the terminology employed by some lawyers: "nonrefundable retainer." If it's nonrefundable, it's not a retainer, but a minimum fee.) I will deposit the $5,000 check directly into my trust account, and the same day I will write a check to myself for $1900 (my minimum fee which has been earned) and I will deposit it into my checking account. When it is time to file the petition for divorce, I will write a check for $202 payable to the district clerk, drawn on my trust account.

HAL S. DAVIS III
ATTORNEY & COUNSELOR
MASTER OF BUSINESS ADMINISTRATION
44⬛44

1700 ALMA DRIVE, SUITE 310 ı PLANO, TEXAS 75075-6936
TEL 972-881-1811 ı *FAX* 972-578-2209 ı DAVIS@PLANOLAW.COM

April 3, 2000

Ms. April Smith
123 Fourth Street
Plano, TX 75023

Dear Ms. Smith:

This is to bill you for my time since my previous bill, and to advise you of the status of your retainer account.

March 1, 2000 initial consultation with client in office; prepare petition for divorce, waiver of citation, and first draft of final decree of divorce

March 2, 2000 file petition; letter to respondent; telephone call with client

March 8, 2000 telephone call with client; telephone call with opposing counsel; telephone call with court coordinator; telephone call with opposing counsel; telephone call with client

March 20, 2000 prepare for temporary orders hearing with client in office

March 21, 2000 temporary orders hearing

March 22, 2000 draft temporary orders; telephone call and letter to client conveying draft temporary orders

March 25, 2000 discuss revisions to temporary orders with client; revise temporary orders; letter conveying temporary orders to opposing counsel

Total time this period 10 hours at $180/hour $1,800	
Previous retainer balance	0
Plus receipts this period (initial retainer)	$5,000
Minus disbursements other than legal fees (filing fee)	-$162.00
Minus disbursements for legal fees	-$1,800.00
New retainer balance	$3,138
Target retainer balance	$3,138
Please remit	$0

We have the temporary orders agreed and signed, and it appears most other matters will fall into place. You must get your draft of the inventory and appraisement to me within the next two weeks. In about a month we will pick a mediator and I expect this will be settled at mediation. Accordingly, I believe the current retainer balance is sufficient at this time.

Please call if you have any questions or problems. I never charge for a telephone call about a bill.

Very truly yours,

Hal S. Davis III

After providing a detailed statement of how much money is earned and how, I may write a check to myself drawn on the trust account, withdrawing $900 of my client's funds (I've earned $1,800, but I've already been paid $900 with the minimum fee, so I'm only due an additional $900).

Interest on Lawyer's Trust Account

Your trust account will earn interest. Technically, each of the deposits you are holding in the account is earning interest individually. That is, if I have 20 clients' money in my trust account and a total of $20,000 in the trust account, and the trust account has earned $20 interest over the last month, I would need to figure out what part of the $20 belongs to each of the 20 clients. The trouble is, for me it's usually more like 35 clients and $11 in interest. Add to that the fact that one client may have $5,000 on deposit and another may have $350. You could easily spend way too much time figuring out how to be fair with the $11.

Many states have passed legislation that save the lawyer from this dilemma by simply taking away the interest and giving it to the poor. In Texas it is called the IOLTA (Interest On Lawyer's Trust Account) program, and the proceeds help provide free legal services to the poor. Each month the bank takes the earned interest back out of your account and sends it to the appropriate authority. To me, this is a blessing. The lesson here, however, is that when you open your bank accounts, you need to be sure that the bank understands your state's legislation on lawyer's trust accounts and has a system set up to comply.

If the nature of your practice is such that you may wind up with really large amounts of money belonging to one client for more than a couple of days, you will want to open a separate account just for that client, and it should not be your local equivalent of an IOLTA account. If the earning potential of the funds will easily exceed the monthly bank charges for an account, you owe your client the duty of making sure that the money you are holding for her is properly invested. This would at least be an interest bearing checking account, but might involve something more involved such as a mutual fund. But beware: lawyers have been sued for malpractice for investing trust funds in investments that dropped significantly in value while in the lawyer's care. Check with your state bar on the ethics and regulations involved.

So what does this have to do with software?

To the bank, the lawyer's trust account has one balance, and it belongs to you, as trustee. Nobody knows how much of what's in that account belongs to which individual client except for you. Every month I see bar disciplinary notices for lawyers who failed to keep client funds separated from their own. You *must* have bookkeeping or accounting software that will help you track how much money you are holding for each client.

There are specialized, lawyer-specific solutions out there, but I have avoided them because they are needlessly complex and expensive for my needs.

There are three software packages that are highly rated by the computer press year after year for reliability and ease of use. They are Peachtree Complete Accounting (www.peachtree.com), Intuit's QuickBooks, and Intuit's Quicken (www.intuit.com).

Peachtree is a full-featured true accounting system, but it is based on double-entry bookkeeping. If you have had a couple of courses in basic accounting and know the difference between a debit and a credit, this is the system I recommend.

QuickBooks is a beefed-up version of Quicken (below). It is more fully featured, but it is not a double-entry bookkeeping system. It has a billing module to help send out bills, but it does not integrate with a time tracking package such as Timeslips (at least, not the last time I checked). I tried using QuickBooks several years ago and found it too awkward to use. The logic of the program simply did not accommodate the concept of a lawyer's trust account (or "retainage"), and I had to set up two different companies, one for my trust account and one for my other accounts. To go from my trust account to my operating account, I had to close out one company and open the other.

The simplest program of the three, and the one I use, is Quicken. The logic of the program is the metaphor of a checkbook. You simply enter every transaction in your checkbook register, telling the program what the check or deposit was for. The trick for a lawyer is to set up a "class" for each client for whom you are going to track retainage (I don't set up a class for a client if they are expected to be a flat-fee case). You can set up reports of transactions by class so that you can see what the retainer balance is for each client.

Quicken does not have a billing module, but does have an accounts receivable module to track whether people on payment plans are paying as agreed. When you print checks, they can be set up to print the payee's address on the check so that you can just drop the checks in special window envelopes and save time addressing bill payments. Quicken and QuickBooks are both from Intuit, the company that makes Turbo Tax income tax preparation software, and you can send your data directly from either bookkeeping package into the tax preparation package. The biggest disadvantage of Quicken is that it produces all expense reports with the categories of income and expense arranged in alphabetical order: "advertising" is shown before "rent" and "software." Anyone who has taken management accounting would arrange the categories differently from this method, but that's not allowed in this software.

Time Tracking and Billing

The oldest and most established time tracking software is Timeslips (www.timeslips.com). This is a very flexible and powerful package that allows you to track and enter time accounting information. It has a stopwatch feature that will run in the background, tracking time spent on one project until you tell it that you've changed projects. It will also produce bills for you to mail to your clients. There is even a version that will run on handheld computers such as the Palm Pilot.

But I don't use a time tracking a billing software package. I record my time in the memo function of my Palm Pilot. This is a simple but effective system, and it works well for me. I use the "shortcut" function to speed data entry. To produce a bill, I just cut and paste the information from my memo into a letter. That's just because most of my cases are flat-fee, and I don't do much time tracking and billing.

There are also other lawyer-specific integrated solutions out there. I'm afraid I have no opinion on any specific product, as I'm satisfied with my current solutions. However, I do have a couple of cautions. Lawyer-specific software tends to be much more expensive than generic business applications. It's more difficult to find trained staff on specialized applications. And, most of the lawyer-specific software is far, far more complex than the average sole practitioner needs.

Spreadsheet

Many lawyers are completely unaware of the power and capabilities of spreadsheet software. In the early days of personal computing, many people bought computers just to run spreadsheet software. It is difficult to explain spreadsheets in such a way as to convey the simplicity and power of the concept, but I will try. First, any sort of financial data can be entered as though you were using a pencil and a large columnar accountant's pad. Information in any location can be easily defined by how it relates to any other location. For example, if you were doing a financial projection on the profitability of a business, February's sales could be quickly set up as whatever January's was, or as 5% more than January's. Subtotals and totals are easy to set up, and in the example, you could change one key item in the projection and immediately see how this changed the overall profitability picture.

Spreadsheets are also widely used as simple databases. While they lack the relational capabilities of true database packages, they offer the tremendous advantage of being straightforward and easy to use. Most of all, they are conceptually easy to understand.

My most frequent use of spreadsheets is in itemizing property to be divided in a divorce. My client will provide me with a list of the assets and liabilities to be divided, along with his or her valuation of the asset. There will be a column for property to be awarded to the husband, and a column for property to be awarded to the wife. During negotiations we can change valuations and change the columns for who gets to keep something, and the impact is immediately seen on the bottom line, with a total of the net assets awarded to each party, along with a calculation of the percentage split.

Spreadsheet programs are also great for analyzing trends in your client database, analyzing a marketing plan for your business, analyzing the expenses of your business, and doing time-value-of-money calculations.

If you aren't already familiar with what a spreadsheet program is and how it works, you really owe it to yourself to take a class at the local community college so you'll understand the simplicity and the power of this type of program.

The most popular spreadsheet program is Microsoft's Excel (www.microsoft.com). It is quite versatile and powerful, and I recommend it. However, there are other excellent spreadsheets available, including Quattro Pro and Lotus 123. Your choice may depend on what comes bundled with your word processing software.

Time Value of Money

This topic doesn't really belong here, but it's somewhat related to spreadsheets, so this is as good a place to put it as any.

If you will ever advise your clients about whether or not to take or make a series of payments over time as compared to cash now, you *must* have a basic understanding of the time value of money to avoid malpractice. This comes up in advising your client about taking a "structured settlement", paying alimony, or taking lump sum for an annuity.

The concept is simple. If I offered you a dollar today or a dollar a year from now, you'd certainly choose the dollar today. We all understand that a dollar today is more valuable than a dollar tomorrow. Banks routinely give people a dollar today in return for the promise of $1.10 or so a year from now. If I was obligated to pay you $1 a year for five years, with the first payment due a year from now, and if I could get 10% simple interest at the bank, I could put $3.79 in the bank right now to cover the future payments, because the interest earned over time would cover the additional money needed by each withdrawal.

Let's take an example. Shortly after I was licensed to practice law, I was representing a man in a divorce who had a pension as a government employee. He was 20 years or so from retirement, and he really didn't want to give up any of his pension. And, his wife wanted money *now,* not when he retired in the far distant future. At mediation I was up against a very experienced attorney, who was completely ignorant about how time value of money analysis works. We prepared an analysis of the present value of the wife's share of the pension. Parts of the analysis were a number of assumptions about interest rates, retirement age, life expectancy, etc. When there was a range of values that could be used, we used a value that was at the end that most favored us. We naturally expected them to negotiate with us about these values, but in their ignorance they accepted our figures at face value, and my client saved tens of thousands of dollars simply because we understood the time value of money.

More specific example: suppose my client expected to retire in 20 years and draw retirement of $6,000 per month for another 20 years, and then fall over dead. We look in the Wall Street Journal, and decide that the appropriate interest rates to use over the next 40 years are in the range of 4% to 6%, compounded monthly. If we use an interest rate of 4%, we'd have to deposit $445,000 now to replace the future pension payments, but if we use 6%, it's only $253,000. Which interest rate do you think we'd use if we represent Husband?

If you'll be advising your client about future sums of money, you need to be sufficiently knowledgeable about time value of money analysis to understand how important it is, and how sensitive it is to the assumptions used. You'll use experts for the complex stuff, but you won't be able to fully use their advice (or cross-examine them!) if you don't understand the basics. This is something you can pick up in a basic finance course at the community college.

Training

Whatever software you choose, you will need to learn to use it. I personally dislike the hyperlinked text of the "help" that comes with software, compared with real users' manuals. I find the treatment of each topic insufficiently detailed, and with all the links that need to be followed, I'm never sure that I've read all the material available on the topic (I'd have to follow each link from each link).

I like the … *for Dummies* series of books only slightly better. I can be sure I have read all the material on a subject, but the treatment is still too breezy for me. Having said that, I will normally buy a … *for Dummies* book when I need to learn a new software package.

When my ignorance is almost complete, or if I am on a short time frame to learn something, I will contact a temporary agency and try to hire their best expert on whatever software

I am trying to learn for a day. This way I pay less than I would have paid for a seminar at a computer center, I get individualized instruction, and we get some of my work done at the same time. But do not watch the temporary work: things will go by so fast that you just don't catch them. You should sit at the computer and have the temporary tell you what to do.

Chapter 15
Utilities and Computer Maintenance

Utilities are computer programs that accomplish a fairly narrow, perhaps rather technical task. The dividing line between applications and utilities is arbitrary. Some utilities are bigger programs than many application software packages, and some are fairly expensive. I won't try to defend why some software bears the title "utility" and some doesn't.

One working definition of "utility" is a small program that should have been part of the operating system and isn't. Even if it becomes part of the operating system, you'll need to know that you have to figure out how to run the task. That would include such functions as disk defragmentation, virus scanning and repair, disk maintenance, and windows registry maintenance. For most of these categories, an excellent, simple solution is the Norton Utilities (www.symantec.com).

Disk defragmentation

As your system writes, reads, and erases files from your hard disk, related files will be strewn about the hard disk in various locations, and even parts of the same file may be in various locations. Imagine a typewritten (not word-processed) document that you are revising. If you whiteout a sentence and type in a new one, the new sentence may be too long to fit in the space occupied by the previous one. You may find yourself typing part of the sentence, then an asterisk, and then you'll type the rest of the sentence on the last page.

Now imagine a phonograph or compact disk with parts of a song scattered into several different places on the surface of the disk. Although the system knows exactly where each bit of information is stored, there is a delay each time the tone arm or read head has to be physically moved from one location to another to access the information. This is called "seek time." When there are a large number of these fragmentations, it takes the computer significantly longer to access information. Enter disk defragmentation.

By periodically running a disk "defragger", say once a month or once a quarter, the utility will rearrange all the information on the hard disk to place all related files close to one another, thereby minimizing the seek time and speeding up the computer.

There is a "defrag" program in Windows. The trick is to mark your calendar to actually run the program periodically. I try to defrag my hard drives every 3 months or so.

Anti-virus

The urge to make one's mark on the world, even in a destructive fashion, is ancient. It certainly predates graffiti. Some folks have made it their life's work to create tiny snippets of malicious code that will wreak havoc on the computers of the world. And all without monetary reward or even bragging rights. This has led to a booming industry in software designed to protect your computer from such malicious code.

Some of these bits of malicious code are viruses, but others are worms, Trojan horses, or other technical terms. The details of how they accomplish their goals are beyond my ken, and beyond the scope of this book, but suffice it to say that if they take root in your computer they will begin reproducing themselves and erasing files on your computer. And if they are given half a chance, they'll the computers of your clients and fellow attorneys.

In order for these naughty bits to propagate, they must implant themselves in communications from one computer to another. Before the Internet, this was by changing the way the computer wrote to floppy disks, so that the naughty bit was part of the information on the disk. Now they can be part of nearly anything communicated over the Internet.

The "Happy 99" worm or virus is an instructive example. I got an email from a friend who often sends me jokes by email. The text of the message was something like, "hope you enjoy!" and attached to it was a file called happy99.exe. Trusting my friend, I executed the file, and was treated to an animated simulation of a fireworks show. It wasn't very interesting, and I wondered why he sent it to me. I erased it and went about my business. What I didn't know is that the program did more than just create a fireworks show. It also wrote itself into my computer in subtler ways. Without me knowing it, my computer began to compose emails from me to people I had sent email to recently. The text of each message was "hope you enjoy!" and attached to each one was a file called happy99.exe. I was sending bad email to folks I knew, and I didn't know I was doing it.

Anti-virus software works in three different ways. First, it will scan the disk to see if it finds any viruses. Second, if it finds a virus it will eradicate it. Third, it will scan anything read from a floppy disk or from the Internet that will be written to the hard disk to quarantine any viruses before they take root. The software matches virus "signatures" to a database of known viruses, so you must update your computer's database periodically. This is a service included with the anti-virus software.

A word of caution. More and more frequently malicious viruses and worms are wreaking great havoc all over the world in a few hours, before anti-virus software routines can be written to detect and remove them. The safe advice is: (1) back up your computer frequently, so if a virus does get loose on your computer, you can put things back the way they were; (2) run anti-virus software frequently and update it frequently; and (3) never, ever open an attachment to an email unless you know and trust the sender *and* you are positive that the sender *intended* to send you that particular file.

Lately I've become disenchanted with Norton Anti-Virus, finding that its roots in my computer are so deep as to be as much of a problem as a simple virus. Currently I use AVG Anti-Virus, from www.grisoft.com. It's simple, fast, and effective. But, I suggest you talk with whoever builds your computer for you for the latest scoop on antivirus software.

Spyware

There is a category of software called Spyware which reports to others what's happening on your computer. The simplest, and most benign form is the "cookie." All things being equal, I like cookies. When I go to check the weather forecast and type in the web address www.wunderground.com, it finds a cookie on my computer that reminds them that my office zip code is 75093, so I get the weather forecast for my local area, without having to remember and type in a much longer address, such as, "http://www.wunderground.com/cgi-bin/findweather/getForecast?query=75093".

But, of course, for every benefit there's a bane. The next level of spyware is merely annoying: you'll buy something on the internet, and the browser will implant something nosier than a cookie that keeps track of all the sites you visit on the internet, so the merchant can decide where to advertise. At this level, it's annoying on principal, because it's none of their business, and also annoying because enough of those programs will slow your computer down.

And, there is also spyware that's effectively a different kind of virus. It'll mess things up on your computer just to give the author/promulgator of the spyware some sort of kick.

To manage this, there are several utilities for finding and removing spyware, and they function much the same way as antivirus software: they need to be updated frequently, and they need to run frequently. As of this writing, I run two different anti-spyware programs: SpyBot Search and Destroy (www.tucows.com), and Ad-Aware (www.lavasoft.com). I believe there's a spyware component in Norton AntiVirus. There are a number of tools available. The trick is to update them and run them periodically, at least monthly.

Internet postage

I like DAZzle (www.envelopemanager.com) for printing postage without a trip to the post office, and without paying for a postage meter. You must be connected to the Internet to print postage, but if you're going to be printing the envelope anyway, you might as well verify the address and print postage on the envelope at the same time. I like this software over the more popular ones, such as stamps.com because DAZzle gives me much more control over the appearance and layout of my mailpieces.

Backup

Until recently, backup was only available in utilities, but it is now part of the operating system. I have found, however, that when I buy a backup device, it will come bundled with backup software that works well with the device. I generally prefer using the backup software that comes with the device.

Adobe Acrobat

Adobe Acrobat is an application that really has no competition (www.adobe.com). When talking about the category, you identify the category simply by naming the product. The concept is to be able to send a document to someone electronically and have it show up on their monitor and their printer exactly as you see it on yours. This is more complicated than it seems, for reasons that delve deeply into the mysteries of operating systems. Part of the problem is with typefaces or fonts, as the person you send a file to may not have the exact same typefaces on her computer. Her system will substitute typefaces, but lines will now end in different places, and pages will break differently. Acrobat provides a way to share typefaces without the hassle of installing more typefaces than you really need, and also without violating the proprietary interests of the typeface "foundry" that sold the typeface to the first person and would have lost a sale to the second person. Adobe also is a major supplier of typefaces, so they want to make it possible to view a document in its native typefaces without sharing illegal copies of the typefaces.

As nearly all of my clients use email, I find it useful to send them draft documents by email. While a WinWord document will almost universally be accepted by them, there are problems. First, if my client has suggested changes to the document, I don't want him to just make the changes and send them back to me, because it will not be clear to me exactly what changes he has made, so I feel there may be malpractice exposure. Second, I may want my client to print out the document, sign it, and return it to me, and I want it to look just like it did in my office.

Adobe Acrobat is just right for this situation. The output at each end is guaranteed to be the same, and the recipient cannot alter the document. Although it is not inexpensive, at over $200, I am surprised at how useful I find it.

Do not be confused with the free Acrobat Reader. While this is free, it only allows you to read Acrobat (.pdf) files, not to create them.

Acrobat will also probably be the key to some innovations we may see in the future such as electronic filing of documents (Acrobat has provisions for electronic signatures).

Chapter 16
Organizing Your Paper Files

There are few things about setting up your law office as boring and yet as crucial as the way you organize your paper files. Being well organized makes the difference in being able to find the client's file when she calls, and making sure that old files don't just get neglected (with the malpractice problems this will cause).

If you practice in more than one area, you should have your files color-coded and separately numbered for each area of practice. Here are some suggestions for color coding:

Green:	Miscellaneous civil
Purple:	Wills and probate
Pink:	Criminal: misdemeanor
Red:	Criminal: felony
Blue:	Family law (divorce)
Orange:	Bankruptcy

There's nothing magic about this system. I originally used red for all criminal matters, until the misdemeanor and felony courts were moved to separate buildings in my home county. I found it convenient to be able to quickly grab all of my misdemeanor files when I was going to the misdemeanor courthouse, and to grab all of my felony files when I went to the other courthouse. Going to different colors for misdemeanors and felonies helped me do that.

If you practice in several counties, you may wish to use different colors for different counties. If you do Chapter 7 and Chapter 13 bankruptcies, you my find it worthwhile to put them in different colored jackets. Or if you do a lot of family law, you may wish to put divorces in one color and non-divorce matters (enforcement, modifications, adoptions, etc.) in another.

I used to type or print my labels for my folders, until I realized I was spending too much time impressing myself. I now simply write the last name of the client and the file number on the tab of the manila folder. I use a very big felt-tip pen ("Sharpie"), but not as big as a Marks-a-Lot. I found that some of my darker-colored manila folders (especially blue) made it hard to read the markings without a label, so I found some colored manila folders from Viking Office Supply (800-421-1222) that were a lighter color on the inside and tab than on the outside.

I like to use a five-digit numbering system for my files. The first two digits are the year, then there's a dash, the next digit indicates the practice area, and the last two digits represent the "serial number" of the file for the year. For example, file number 05-822 would be the 22nd family law (8 = family law) case I opened in the year 2005. This system offers a number of advantages. If you file them numerically, it's easy to see at a glance in your file drawer which files are older: they are the ones in front just glaring at you. Also, when you move files to storage it makes it easier to find an old file. You may have five boxes for a given year, but only one or two will be in the subject area you are trying to find, so it will narrow your search. The only real drawback I have found is when you open more than 100 files of a certain type in a calendar year. If you expect to open a several hundred files of one type in a year, you can simply add another digit to the numbering system. If you figure you could exceed 100 but are unlikely to exceed 200, you can simply skip the next 100 in assigning numbers. In my example, I don't use the 900 series of numbers, so if I opened more than 100 family law cases in a year I could name the next one 00-901 and everything would be fine.

In the lateral file by my desk, I file matters alphabetically by client name. But when I closed the matter and move the file to the big filing cabinet, I filed them by file number.

Again, there's nothing magic to my system, but here's the numbering system I use:

100:	Miscellaneous civil
200:	Criminal: Misdemeanor
300:	Criminal: Felony
400:	Wills and Probate

700:	Bankruptcy
800:	Family

When you start a new year, get a fresh box of colored manila folders for each area of practice and take a moment with a pencil and put serial numbers on the outside of the jacket of each folder. I don't put it on the tab, just in a convenient spot on the jacket. Then, when I open a new file, I don't have to research to determine what the next number is. I grab my Sharpie, write the client's last name, the last two digits of the year, a dash, the number for the type of law, and the two-digit number scribbled on the jacket.

When you enter the data on the new client into your database on your computer, put the file number in its own field. That way, if someone calls you years later and has a question about the case, you find the person in your database, and then you'll have the file number so you can pull it out of storage. I use a Palm Pilot for my client database, and because all my clients are individuals instead of businesses, I use the "title" field for my client file number.

Do not use the case numbers assigned by the local courts. They are much bigger than you need. You'll want your file numbers sequential, so that you can tell quickly whether or not a file is missing. And if court-assigned docket numbers are called "file numbers" in your jurisdiction, then refer to the numbers you put on your files as "case numbers" or anything different to avoid confusion.

I like having a two-drawer lateral filing cabinet close enough to my desk that I can reach it without getting out of my chair. Lateral files hold more files per drawer than regular files, and they don't project into the room as far. Two-drawer lateral files are available in wood to complement the rest of your office furniture. In the top drawer I keep my current (open) files.

You'll need to keep records of all your consultations, and I have a file for the consultation forms, with my notes on the back of each. If the person you consult with hires you, that form goes into the client file. If they do not hire you, or until they hire you, it goes into a separate file of folks you have consulted with. I have a Pendaflex Hanging Expandable File (No. 59225) with dividers for ABC, DEF, GH, and so forth to keep the consultation forms, and I put it in the top drawer of my lateral file, behind the open client files. I'll refer to these if the client comes in later to hire me, to keep track of referral sources and advertising, and to use as notes if there's a grievance or malpractice claim filed. Every year I move all of the consultation sheets into a regular manila folder, and start over again with the divider file.

The bottom drawer of my lateral file holds copies of paid bills, my malpractice insurance policy, the lease agreement for my office, and the like.

When I closed a file, I moved it into a four-drawer metal lateral file in the copy room. I find that if someone calls me about a closed case, it will almost always be within two years of closing the file, and I'm likely to have the file handy. Whenever the four-drawer file became full, I pulled out the oldest files, put them in storage boxes, and took them home to my garage. If this gets to be a storage problem, I'll begin destroying old files. You'll probably be safe destroying files more than four years old, but I'd play it safe and double that. Never destroy files for clients that have had you prepare a will: part of the service you provide is backup in case the original will is accidentally destroyed.

Going Paperless (for archives, anyway)

Having practiced law about 13 years, I have grown weary of old files taking over my garage. With recent advances in scanner technology, the growth of hard drives on computers, and other factors, I've begun scanning and shredding my closed files instead of sending them to storage. Here are some pointers:

- Consider scanning to .pdf (Adobe Acrobat) files, as this increases the probability that you'll be able to read the file years from now (I wouldn't want to try to figure out how I would read an old WordStar word processing file).

- Get a sheet-fed scanner designed for archiving paper files because of their durability, ease of use, and speed. I have a Visioneer scanner rated at 8 pages per minute that cost me $300. I now wish I had paid $700 and gotten the one rated at 20 pages per minute. If you are investigating a new copier, look into a digital copier, which will incorporate a high-speed scanner.

- I don't scan documents that I generated on my computer (because they're already archived, probably as the .pdf file I sent to my client), nor do I scan documents filed with the court. I do scan workpapers, notes and correspondence from my client and from counsel.

- I shred nearly everything after scanning, but particularly anything with social security numbers, drivers license numbers, credit card numbers, and bank account numbers.

- At years' end, I scan all the consultation forms for the folks who didn't hire me.

- I usually scan documents at 200 dots per inch, black and white (not gray, not color). The biggest file I've archived in the last month was 42 pages, and it takes up about 1.1 megabytes of disk space, which comes to about 28 kilobytes per page. The math is a little screwy (because a kilobyte isn't 1000 bytes), but a 60 gigabyte hard drive should be able to hold something in the neighborhood of 2 million pages (without compression).

- One of the biggest advantages of scanning your old files is that you can now back them up, increasing the likelihood that you'll still have them even if a disaster strikes your office.

Chapter 17
Organizing Your Electronic Files

I know a couple of lawyers who developed some habits in the early days of personal computing, and haven't updated their practices. When a client matter is closed, they will copy all of the client files to a floppy disk, drop the floppy into the client folder, and delete the files from the hard disk.

This made some sense when the habit was developed. The first personal computer hard drives were expensive and small (10 megabytes), and floppy disks were the medium used for backups anyway.

Modern personal computer hard drives are over a thousand times as large as the first ones, and we use other media for backup. While *program* files have gotten much larger, requiring much more disk space, the *document* files that lawyers create are about the same size as they were years ago. This entire book is stored in a word processing file smaller than a half a megabyte. The average client letter takes up less than 50 kilobytes of disk space. Even a fairly complicated Texas divorce decree with children, over 40 pages at 1½ line spacing only takes up about 100 kilobytes, or a tenth of a megabyte. If each of your client files had 20 outgoing letters and five 30-page pleadings that you prepared in it, a 10 gigabyte hard disk could store the information on over 6,000 clients. Floppy disks are now comparatively expensive on a cost per byte stored basis. Moving client files off of your hard disk is neither necessary nor advisable.

I advise you to keep every single file, document, and letter you ever create on your hard disk on your computer, and then to perform regular backups of the drive. I guarantee that you will want to find a document from an old matter, and it will be much, much faster and easier to find it on the computer than trying to dig the paper file out of archives. Even if the paper file is within arm's reach, it will be much handier to pull the file up on your computer so you can copy the file and begin editing it.

Using the utilities I write about in another chapter, you can even find old documents when you don't even remember the name of the client.

Storage costs have now gotten so low that in many larger firms all *incoming* documents and pleadings are scanned and stored on the computer as well, and the paper file is never removed from the archives. Optical Character Recognition ("OCR") software converts the image to searchable text. Lawyers needing to see the "file" just pull them up on their computer screens, and can print an exact image of the original document if they need to. This is the way to go if multiple lawyers are working on a file, as nobody has to fight over possession of the paper file.

Scanning all documents also makes sense when there are hundreds or thousands of documents in a matter. It is so much easier to pull up the needed document on the computer than it is to search through boxes in the war room.

But scanning documents for online storage is more time, effort, and expense than it's worth for the average new solo lawyer. It takes no time at all to drop the incoming letter or pleading into the file. Disregarding the hardware and software costs, it would take you several extra minutes to scan a document and run the OCR software to get it stored in your computer. Plus, when you got to the courthouse or mediation session, you would need to have the paper document anyway.

You need a logical way of quickly finding the documents you have created. I use a simple system that works very well for me. It is based on nested folders, with more particularity as I go deeper into the system. Start with a single folder called "Documents" or "My Documents" or whatever makes sense for you. You want this folder to contain nothing but documents you have created (that is, it should not contain any programs) so that backups and searches can be restricted to a small portion of the computer.

Within my "Documents" folder I have several more folders, including one for each general area of law that I practice. I have folders for bankruptcy, civil law, criminal law, family law, and wills. I also have a folder named "x_other" and "z_correspondence." The last two are named as they are so that they appear at the end of my list of folders.

Within each general practice area, I have a folder for each client, plus a folder named "z_closed." If John Smith hires me to do a divorce, I will create a new folder named "SmithJohn" in my family law folder. When the divorce is over, I will use Windows Explorer to move Mr. Smith's folder into the z_closed folder within family law. Now when I need to open a family law file, I only see a list of the open files, but I can quickly get to a closed file if I need to. The system looks like this:

```
documents
        bankruptcy
        civlaw
        crimlaw
        famlaw
                AdamsWF
                BakerJD
                        decree
                        ltr to clerk – file petn
                        ltr to client re whatnot
                        ltr bill to client
                        petn
                        tempord
                        waiver
                CooperFS
                x_corresp
                z_closed
                        DavisBR
                        EdwardsJF
        wills
        x_other
        z_corresp
```

I use the x_other folder for projects I do that are not for clients, such as for a club I'm a member of, or a book I'm writing. I use the z_correspondence folder for letters that have nothing to do with any particular client, such as a letter to the telephone company or to the people who print my business cards. I use the x_corresp folder within a given practice area for correspondence that does have to do with that practice area, but not with any given client, such as a letter to a prospective client.

It's generally easy to give descriptive names to the pleadings in a client file, such as "Petition for Divorce" or "Second Amended Motion for Sanctions." It's a bit more difficult for the letters you create on a matter. I usually start the names of all letters with "ltr" so they'll all appear together when I sort the directory alphabetically.

In Windows, you'll find it handy to note that when you're looking at a list of files, you can click on the headings of the various columns, and the list will be sorted according to that column. That is, if you click on the column heading for the names of the files, the files will appear in order of their names, alphabetically. If you click on the column heading for "date modified," you'll see it sorted by date.

Chapter 18
Computer
Maintenance

There are a few tasks you should perform on your computer periodically to keep everything operating smoothly. The tasks are neither complicated nor time-consuming, but your computer won't do these automatically (yet).

Backup

Backing up your computer's files is boring and tedious. The fact that you need the backed up data so seldom makes it easy to be lulled into indifference about doing regular backups. But you *will* need your backup someday, and the only question is how old your backup is, and therefore how much data you lose. In the twenty-five years I have been using personal computers, I have had my hard disk "crash" resulting in lost data only three times. Hard disks have moving parts and they will wear out or break down. Computers are stolen from offices, and natural disasters strike lawyers with about the same frequency as they do the rest of the population.

But I've also changed a document, saved it, and then wished I could go back to the version I started with. With a recent backup, it will only take a couple of minutes to restore the version you had before the last backup.

Most of the data on your computer is information that would be very inconvenient to lose, but a very little of it would be nearly catastrophic to lose. It helps to categorize the information in order to plan a backup strategy.

The first category of information on your disk is software. Program files take up a huge portion of the space on your hard disk, and although it would take time and money to replace them, they are by no means irreplaceable. Besides, you should have a box in your storeroom with all the boxes and disks for the software programs on your computer.

The second category is junk. Your computer creates a huge amount of data that it uses to keep track of what it's doing and what it has done, but the information can be replaced without you knowing it was ever lost in the first place. This includes temporary files (frequently with a name ending in .tmp) and caches of sites visited on the Internet. These should never be backed up, as it would take more time to restore the old ones than for the computer to automatically recreate them from scratch.

Then there are configuration files. When you install software, you spend a considerable amount of time telling it how you want it to work for you. You tell your word processor what typefaces you like to use, and you tell your document assembly software what rules to use to create documents. This also applies to the Windows operating system, with its registry of how you set up your computer.

These files can all be replaced, but not with money: it requires tedious hours of you sitting in front of the computer telling the software how you want it to run.

If you have been computing for a while, there is a considerable amount of fluff on your computer. From wallpaper to sounds to long-forgotten games, there is information that you could lose without shedding a tear, and you would probably not bother to replace it.

Then there's ordinary data: letters, pleadings, spreadsheets, and memoranda. You'd hate to lose these, even on a really old case, but you could carry on without them if you had to, particularly if your paper file wasn't destroyed in the same fire/tornado/flood/explosion/burglary that destroyed your computer. These should be backed up regularly, but not necessarily daily, and a copy of the backup should be kept off site.

Finally there's the information that's just irreplaceable. I can think of only two types of information in this category: information that I keep in my Palm Pilot (calendar, phone book, and to-do), and data used by my accounting software. Without my calendar I would miss court dates and I could lose my license. Without detail on how much money I have in my trust account that belongs to what client, I could lose my license.

The key to having a backup to bail you out is making frequent backups and storing the data in a place that is unlikely to be affected by the same disaster that destroyed the computer. The key to frequent backups is convenience: if it's a hassle to do a backup, you won't do them.

A while back I toyed with using a removable hard disk for my backup. Backup should have been much faster to a hard disk than to nearly any other medium, so I tried it. But I lost sight of the real lesson. The key was convenience, not speed. At the time, my removable hard disks held a gigabyte ("GB") of data, and my non-removable hard disk held about 3 GB. I could start a backup, go to lunch, and come back to find that the 1 GB disk was full. But then I'd have to replace the disk to let the backup resume, and I'd be unproductive at my desk while the backup continued.

The mainstay backup medium is tape. Although tape backup is comparatively slow, you can generally buy tapes big enough to hold the entire contents of your hard disk, and this makes backup as convenient as it gets. You start a backup when you leave the office for the day, and when you come in the next morning you just pop the backup tape into your briefcase.

Two types of backups you'll need to know about are "full" and "incremental" backups. A full backup backs up just about everything on your hard disk, although you can configure it to exclude junk and fluff that never need to be backed up. An incremental backup is a backup of only those files that have been added or changed since the last backup. A full backup may be gigabytes in size and take a couple of hours to perform. An incremental backup may only be a few megabytes and take only ten minutes to perform.

I suggest that you do a full backup at least monthly, and preferably weekly. Start the backup when you leave the office and remove the tape when you come in the next morning. Whenever you do a full backup, put the tape in a desk drawer, and take the previous full backup out of the drawer and put it in your briefcase. This affords some protection if a disaster wreaks havoc on both your computer and the tape in your desk drawer.

In the time between full backups do incremental backups frequently. Any time you create a particularly complex or difficult document, do an incremental backup before you leave the office. Or, if you're only doing full backups monthly, do an incremental backup at least weekly.

You should also do smaller, quicker, very targeted backups even more frequently on the information that it would be catastrophic to lose. If you use a handheld computer, such as a Palm Pilot, every time you synchronize it with the desktop computer you have backed up the data. All that remains for me is to back up my accounting software's data at least daily. I use Quicken, and my data files can be backed up to floppy disks (or a Zip drive) in less than a minute, which I used to do every time I used my accounting software (but now I use Internet backup).

Internet backup

I've been using internet backup for several years now and I am sold. You download backup software from the Internet and install it on your computer. Then you transfer backup data via the Internet to your backup service's computer.

Using encryption, this can be quite secure, and your backup data will always be in a secure, remote location unlikely to be affected by whatever disaster befell your computer. And you may set the system up to allow you access to your data anywhere you have access to a computer, such as at a friend's office while your computer is being replaced.

One of the biggest advantages of Internet backup is that you don't have to remember to drop a tape into the machine and start a backup. As long as you remember to leave your computer on overnight, you can schedule a backup to happen while you are sleeping.

The two biggest concerns with Internet backup are paying for the space to store your backup and the time to send your information over telephone lines. Storage prices have been plummeting for many years now, and it is not very expensive to rent sizable storage on a remote computer.

The time to transmit data is also decreasing as higher speed Internet becomes more widely available and less expensive. Sending a gigabyte of data over a dialup connection may take 40 hours, but using a high-speed DSL line it might only take 4 hours. Also, advances in compression and file comparison technology allow incremental backups to be transmitted in a few minutes.

I now use connected.com online backup. Since I started scanning closed files, my storage needs have grown significantly, but I still pay only $25 per month to protect as much as 10 gigabytes of data. The system automatically backs up anything on my computer that has changed. It backs up at random times during the night, and most days the backup takes less than five minutes. I do have DSL high-speed internet, but it is ADSL (the first letter is for Asynchronous) meaning that the download speed and upload speed are different. My upload speed isn't much faster than dialup.

Recently it has become quite economical to store information on other computers, such as through Google's email service, but backing up data to them is a manual process (you decide which files, individually, to back up, and you transfer them to the remote storage).

For more information, start your search with www.connected.com.

Delete unneeded files

At least once a month you should right-click on your recycling bin on your desktop and delete the contents. The recycling bin is a place for deleted files that allows you to rethink your decision to delete them. But sooner or later the files need to be deleted.

You should also run a utility such as Clean Sweep, part of the Norton Utilities, to identify useless files that need to be deleted. If you're not sure whether or not they can be deleted, leave them on the disk.

Search for disk problems

Also at least once per month you should run a disk analysis program such as Norton Disk Doctor to see if there any problems with the hard disk. Most problems are fixed by the analysis software, and if there is a serious problem the software will alert you.

Defragment the hard disk

After your monthly deletion of unneeded files and checking the disk for problems, you should run a disk defragmentation utility, such as Norton Speed Disk or defrag.exe (which comes with Windows).

Chapter 19
Forms

One of the first lawyers to come to my seminar had been practicing law for about a year and had been experiencing good success in attracting clients. But his record keeping was chaotic at best. During the course of the initial interview, if it occurred to him, he would ask the client for his telephone number and the lawyer would write it in the margin of the legal pad he was making notes in. If he needed more information later, he would have to call the client and ask.

There are two basic types of forms for the lawyer: legal practice forms and office management forms. Legal practice forms are such things are divorce forms, deed forms, will forms, and the other types of documents you prepare for your client. I will not address those, as your choice will be dictated by your practice areas, the state in which you are licensed, cost, and personal preference. I suggest you talk to other lawyers in your field and get their opinions.

Office management forms are those forms you will need for the business of managing your law practice. Nobody enjoys forms, but most clients would rather fill out a form one time than have you calling them over and over again for the information you need. Forms can save you from grievances and malpractice.

As you read your state's bar journal or other publications, and particularly if you get a newsletter from your malpractice insurance carrier, you will see recurring themes and interesting cases. For example, I remember reading a case about a woman who came to see a lawyer, talked about her lawsuit, and left. The woman said that she had hired the lawyer and he failed to respond to the lawsuit, resulting in a default judgment against the woman. The lawyer said that he was never hired. The woman responded that she had left the papers with which she was served in the lawyer's office, and she would not have done that if she had not hired the lawyer. The court found in favor of the woman. As a result, my client consultation form has a statement that no legal services will be performed after the initial consultation without a written agreement.

First I collect all of the usual information: full legal name, nickname, address, and phone numbers. Then, because the pleadings I prepare often require it, I will ask for date of birth, social security number, and driver's license number. I will also ask for fax numbers, mobile phone numbers, pager numbers, and email addresses.

I am also concerned that I will leave a message for my client in a manner that is not confidential, resulting in embarrassment or loss to my client. So I ask my client to specify how I may leave confidential messages. That way, if a message is intercepted, I can tell my client that she authorized leaving messages at that number.

It's also important to me to be able to track where I get my new clients, so on my consultation form I will ask how they got my name, and whether I may call that person and thank them.

The bottom third of the intake form is some information I give to the client, and at the bottom I ask the client to sign and date it, acknowledging receipt of the information. As I said, I tell the client that no work will be performed without a written agreement. Then I have a statement required by the State Bar of Texas about how to file a grievance against a lawyer. Finally I tell the client in writing how much the initial consultation will cost (such as $90 for the first half hour, and $45 per quarter hour or portion thereafter, to a maximum of two hours). If the client was not expecting to pay for the consultation, I find out before the consultation, not afterward. I always have the client complete and sign the consultation form before I begin the consultation.

I have also developed a different consultation form for divorce. In addition to the information on the basic consultation form, this form asks for the spouse's full legal name, date of birth, social security number, and so on, and similar information on the children. I will ask who has the children now, whether the spouse is represented by counsel, whether there are retirement accounts that may need to be split, whether there is any real estate, what cars are involved, whether there has been violence in the marriage, and much more. When feasible, I like to email, fax, or mail the form to the client before the consultation to give them a chance to gather the necessary information.

I recommend that you talk with a number of lawyers, and ask each one for a sample consultation form, and ask the lawyer why unusual information is listed. You will develop a great deal of useful information, and you will make friends with some interesting people. Buy them lunch if you feel guilty.

While you're talking with the other lawyers, ask them for copies of the engagement letters or contracts. You can also get similar forms in the practice area form books at your local law library.

When designing your engagement letters or forms, you will want to try to keep them brief. Aside from irritating potential clients, you'll want a jury to believe that the client actually read and understood the entire document before they signed it.

One of the most interesting forms I have seen is a specially printed manila case file jacket, with room for all kinds of information. I don't like having too much information on the outside of a jacket, because I am concerned about client confidentiality if someone else sees the jacket at the courthouse.

I do like to print large mailing labels with checklists on them to put on the outside of a jacket. On bankruptcies I will have checkboxes for whether the client has returned the information forms I gave them, whether I have drafted pleadings, whether the client has reviewed the pleadings, when the case was filed, when the first meeting of creditors was scheduled, and whether the trustee required additional information.

On criminal matters, I will record the plea bargain negotiations directly on the front cover of the jacket. I will put down whether the client wants a trial or wishes to plead guilty. Then I will put the offer from the state including any special conditions requested, or unexpected evidence I am told about. If the client decides to go to trial, there will be a wealth of information in the file, but most of my cases have most of the necessary information recorded on the outside of the jacket.

I will also use the outside of the jacket to make notes to myself about the progress of the case or any other special concerns. These notes may be "don't leave messages on home machine," or "waiting on QDRO pre-approval from employer," or "attach copy of NSF check to motion for enforcement."

There are no rules on forms. Design them and change them as you see fit to assure that you gather the information you need and, and to remind you of the things you need to do.

Chapter 20
That First
Phone Call

The first telephone call with a prospective client is vital. You must convey and receive so much vital information in a couple of minutes that it is important to be prepared.

Once you have chatted enough about what they are looking for to determine that you can help them, jump right to the key question: when would you like to come in? Unless the person needing to hire you is hundreds of miles away, do not attempt to conduct the initial interview over the telephone. Aside from the form you need to have them sign before the consultation, it is unlikely that you will be paid for your time if the potential client is not in your office. Sure, there are workarounds, such as faxing or emailing a consultation form, and accepting a credit card over the telephone, but unless large distances are involved, it's best to just have the potential client come into the office.

Unless the client has a real sense of urgency, try to put the first consultation off for a couple of days. First, this allows you to send them whatever forms they need to complete before the consultation. Second, you want to create the impression that your time is valuable and they cannot just drop in with any hope of finding you available.

Suggest a specific date and time, "I'm available at 11:30 on Thursday." Indeed, your calendar may have nothing on it for the entire week, but you don't have to let the potential client know that. Let them counter with a different date or time (which may, remarkably, be one when you're available).

I suggest that you think twice before you book appointments outside of your normal business hours. My experience is that those that take their affairs seriously will make the time to see you during office hours. I found that the more accommodating I was in seeing someone after hours or on weekends, the more likely I was to be stood up. You may be able to avoid this problem if you require them to confirm the appointment with a credit card.

As soon as you and the potential client have agreed on a date and time, you should begin typing the required information into your calendar software. First, type the client's name and the subject matter. Ask how they got your name: the memory is fresh now, and you'll never have as good a chance to find out what relationships or advertising are working for you.

Ask for a telephone number "in case I am called to court." You do not want to give the impression that you are casual about breaking this important appointment, but you also have to make it clear that sometimes things change and you need to let them know.

Give them directions to office, and tell them what to bring. If you need to email or fax forms to them, get their email address or fax number.

Your entry in your calendar software should look something like this: March 1, 10:00: Bill Johnson re div from Dallas LRS $20 972-578-1234 bjohnson@aol.com."

When you have the information in the calendar, you need to have a closing spiel. Mine would go something like this: "OK, I have you down for Thursday at 10:00 in my office. Bring the forms I'll be emailing to you. Because you were referred by the Dallas Lawyer Referral Service, the charge for your first half-hour consultation is only $20. If you need to change or cancel the appointment, please just call and let me know. If you don't call and you don't come, there is a $35 broken appointment fee. Any questions?"

One restaurant found that it considerably reduced the number of people who failed to show up for their appointments with one simple to their script at the end of the reservation call. While formerly they said, "… and you'll need to call us if your plans change," they changed it to, "… and can we count on you to call us if your plans change?"

Everybody loves getting a special deal. When the potential client arrives, I will manually cross out the "usual" fee for the first half hour and hand write the "special" price. I only lower the price for the first half hour, and keep the usual hourly rate if the consultation takes longer than usual.

My general advice is not to offer free consultations. I have found that my best clients value my time and are willing to pay. If the first question out of a caller's mouth is whether I offer a free consultation, they are unlikely to be a good client. However, I do sometimes print coupons for free consultations and put them in advertising. For the coupon to have value, the recipient must believe that persons without the coupon will have to pay. I would much rather charge $20 for a consultation and give the money to charity than give free consultations, because I am much more likely to wind up with a good client if they have paid for the consultation.

A quick word about conducting the initial interview with the client. During an initial half-hour consultation, try to say very little, except for asking questions, for the first twenty minutes. Of course, if the client asks questions, try to answer them. But if the client wants to tell a long, rambling story about how he got in this mess, it's his nickel and you shouldn't interrupt. They will not think of the money you're saving them if you interrupt with questions trying to lead them to the point. You should tell them when the first half hour is almost over and ask them if they want to continue, clearly implying that it's going to cost more than the half-hour consultation rate you quoted them.

Remember that you are an attorney and counselor, and the second part is more than just telling the client what the law is. Listen carefully to what the client says the problem is, and determine what outcome they would like. Carefully evaluate whether their hopes are realistic. Consider turning away clients if you do not think you will be able to achieve their goals.

If you do think the client's desired outcome is achievable, be careful to manage his or her expectations. It's difficult to settle a case with a happy client if you told her she has a million-dollar claim in the initial interview and then tell her it's worth $50,000 at mediation.

Chapter 21
Insurance

The most obvious insurance for a lawyer is malpractice insurance. The policy I have offers $100,000 per claimant, and $300,000 per incident, with a $5,000 deductible. The price I have paid over the last several years has ranged between $1,000 and $2,000 per year.

Many lawyers choose to not purchase malpractice insurance because they feel that being insured invites a lawsuit or claim. My opinion is that if I do make a mistake that results in a loss for my client, I'd like for some money to be available to make them whole. And I'd also like someone else to pay for the attorney to defend me against a frivolous claim. But a more pragmatic reason for having malpractice insurance is that many lawyer referral services will not allow you to be listed unless you provide proof of at least $100,000 in malpractice coverage.

The cost and availability of malpractice coverage for a given individual or firm depends not only on the amount of coverage and the deductible, but also on whether you were covered during the preceding year, your practice areas, your claims experience, and their records of losses to attorneys in the last few years. Some of it you can control, some you cannot. I used to apply to several carriers each year, but I found that one particular agency always had the best deal for me, and I no longer apply elsewhere, partly because the application forms are so long and tedious.

Some of the questions on the application forms do not seem to make sense in a one-person firm. For example, you may see a question like, "Does the firm have a policy on serving on boards of clients?" Your first reaction may be no, the firm has no policies. Your second reaction should be that as a general rule it's probably a bad idea to serve on the board of a client, and besides, your clients haven't asked you to, yet. So your third reaction should be to type up a statement that it is the firm's policy that lawyers shall not serve on the boards of clients without prior approval from the proprietor. Meaning, of course, that you can't serve on a board unless you think it's a good idea. Attach the page to the application packet, and check the box saying you do have such a policy.

To find malpractice agents, talk to lawyers in your area, and look for ads in bar publications.

If you are renting space from a commercial landlord, you may be required to have premises liability insurance. This covers such things as slip and fall accidents in your space, as well as something electrical in your space having a disastrous failure and damaging someone else's equipment elsewhere in the building. I paid about $50 per year for my policy. I am not currently required to have this insurance, and I do not carry it. If you need it, talk to a homeowner's insurance carrier, preferably the agent that insures your home.

You may also be interested in contents insurance, which will buy you a new desk, filing cabinet, and computer if the building blows up. This is also available from a homeowner's insurance company.

You may be interested in an umbrella liability coverage policy. These pick up the liability coverage where your homeowner's, premises liability, and automobile liability policies stop and bring your total coverage to several millions of dollars. These may or may not extend your malpractice coverage as well. They are not very expensive, and may be a good value if you have significant assets to protect, or if you have exposure to a very large judgment. Talk to a homeowner's insurance agent.

Health insurance is very difficult to obtain economically for the solo lawyer. The ideal situation is to be married to someone that works for a large corporation with excellent health benefits. But if you have not married well, do not despair: even if you pay significantly more for health insurance, it shouldn't cost so much to make you abandon your dreams of being self-employed. There are all kinds of groups for health insurance. Look for groups like your state bar association, the American Bar Association, your local city or county bar association, your state family/criminal/probate bar associations, your local chamber of commerce, your school's alumni association, and so on. And if are married, check for organizations he or she may belong to that offer health insurance.

You may wish to investigate employee leasing. In my particular case The Davis Law Firm told its leasing company, Administaff, Inc., that it needed a lawyer. Administaff hired an attorney that was referred to them named Hal. Each month The Davis Law Firm paid Administaff for providing employees. Each month Administaff paid its employee Hal a fair wage. Hal had a fairly complete menu of affordable health insurance options available through his big employer, Administaff. At the end of the year, Hal had only to attach his W-2 from his employer to his tax return. Hal also owns a law business, but it always seems to just break even after payroll expenses. All health benefits were paid with pre-tax dollars, and Administaff even had a 401(k) retirement plan available. Since I made this arrangement, however, most employee leasing companies have stopped taking new clients with less than five employees, and eventually the leasing company failed to renew my contract because they required at least three employees, even to renew existing clients

If anyone besides you is counting on your income to pay bills, you need life insurance. This area is unduly complicated and consumer unfriendly. You'll ask a simple question like, "How much will it cost me each month to make sure that my widow gets $250,000 on my death?" The answer will take all evening, and will include discussions of term life, whole life, universal life, cash surrender value, dividend reinvestments, and coverage of premiums. Sometimes I think I'd get a clearer answer if I went to Las Vegas and talked to a sports bookie. I want to scream that I don't want a cash surrender value, I just want to pay X dollars a month until I die, at which time my widow gets the money we discussed. But I digress. There are dozens, perhaps hundreds, of books, pamphlets, flyers, and web sites dedicated to understanding the imponderables of life insurance. Expect a telephone call from an old high school classmate trying to set up an appointment to talk with you about life insurance.

At least as important to the young lawyer is disability insurance. There is short-term disability designed to cover your office expenses and a certain portion of your normal paycheck while you recuperate from a major surgery or accident. Long-term disability assumes that you were hurt badly enough that you will no longer be practicing law and you have eliminated your office expenses and just need a portion of your former paycheck to buy groceries and help with the mortgage. While disability coverage will be significantly more expensive than life insurance, you are also far more likely to be disabled before retirement age than you are to die. Disability insurance is almost as complicated as life insurance, but instead of being needlessly complicated because the products are poorly designed from a consumer viewpoint (life insurance), it just takes a while to properly customize disability coverage to fit your needs and budget. Ask around to find a true disability insurance specialist.

Chapter 22
Retirement Planning

Retirement planning for lawyers is either simpler or more complex than for other people, depending on your viewpoint. As a solo, you are not going to have a pension plan like the mailman does, or even a 401(k) plan like the clerk at the local Wal-Mart. But lawyers also tend to work, perhaps on a diminished basis, much later in life than other people. Thus, if lawyers have enough disability insurance, they may be able to make do with much less in the way of retirement benefits.

Personal injury lawyers have certain advantages. Settlements may be "structured" to pay the client the settlement proceeds over many years. If the client's settlement is structured, the attorney's contingent fee may be structured as well. For example, the lawyer may choose to have $10,000 per year come in for four years when the lawyer's child reaches college age. Or the lawyer may structure the settlement into an annuity beginning when the lawyer reaches age 65. Of course, structuring a payday for the future also means that the lawyer must give up the payday today.

Lawyers who don't practice personal injury have the options available to any small businessperson. You just have to set aside some of your earnings and invest it. Tax regulations change frequently, but there are a number of plans to investigate, such as Individual Retirement Accounts ("IRA's"), Roth IRA's, and Keogh Plans.

A "regular" IRA is an account into which you invest before-tax money, usually with an annual limitation on how much can be contributed. You don't pay income tax on the money when you earn it, and you don't pay tax on the increases in value due to appreciation or interest earnings. But when you retire and begin making withdrawals, your withdrawals are ordinary income and you pay income tax on them. However, you hope that you will be in a much lower tax bracket at that time. Also, any withdrawals you make before retirement age carry a 10% penalty and taxes are due. The biggest problem with IRA's is that you are limited to about $2,000 in contributions per year, which makes it difficult to put aside enough to make a real difference in retirement.

A Roth IRA is different. You pay tax on your earnings before you invest them in the Roth IRA, but all of the contents of the Roth IRA are now characterized as after-tax money, so you don't have to pay any tax when you begin making withdrawals at retirement age. You also may contribute significantly more each year.

There are also small-business versions of retirement plans more or less like bigger companies offer. One is called the Simplified Employee Pension plan ("SEP"). SEP's are easy to set up at a bank or brokerage firm. You have to cover all of your permanent employees, if any, but keep in mind that you can also rent employees from temporary agencies, for years on end if you wish.

Keogh plans take a bit more paperwork to establish, but allow more flexibility in setting plan details, such as whether the percentage of earnings contributed to the plan remain the same each year or vary according to your whim and the business profitability. While SEP's do not provide for any vesting period for benefits, a Keogh plan can provide for a vesting period or not.

Whatever investment vehicle you choose, start making contributions to your retirement this year. Because of the magic of compound interest, it is more important to make significant contributions now than it is to make huge investments later.

I'm not a stockbroker or financial advisor, but I can give you some basic information to begin your own research. You have a number of options on managing your investments. Most investments suffer from over-management. Even with lower and lower brokerage fees, frequent trading can erase much of the profits you would otherwise have.

A classic investment strategy book is *A Random Walk Down Wall Street* by Burton Malkiel. The author found that if you picked ten stocks by throwing a dart at the financial section of the newspaper and then just held onto those stocks for ten or twenty years, you would outperform the majority of professional money managers. It's not that professional money managers are lousy at picking good stocks to buy, it's that they buy and sell stocks too frequently. Indeed, there are hundreds of ways to pick good stocks to buy, but very few effective ways to figure out when to sell it. Mr. Malkiel basically says that the best time to sell the stock is after you retire when you need the money.

If retirement is several years away for you, you should invest all of your retirement funds in the stock market. Over the last 200 years or so, stocks have always performed at nearly double the rate for any other type of investment.

Initially it will be difficult for you to diversify your comparatively small investment. It is generally not cost-effective to buy stocks in quantities smaller than 100 shares, and with an average stock price of around $30 per share, a $3,000 investment is necessary for each stock. You will want to diversify into at least ten different stocks, so if one stock turns into a loser it will not have a huge impact on your portfolio, so you must invest $30,000 or so to have a fairly diversified portfolio. Of course, stocks have prices from less than $1 per share (called "penny stocks") to well over $100 per share. If you are trying to manage your own diversified portfolio, you may have to stay away from the more expensive stocks, and buy relatively more of the less expensive stocks. That is, to balance your $3,000 investment in 100 shares of a $30 stock, you should invest $3,000 or so in another stock, and if the second stock were selling for $15 per share, you'd buy 200 shares.

Diversification in your portfolio means diversification of industries. A stock portfolio containing nothing but Internet stocks will do very poorly indeed if Internet stocks as a group experience a price decline. A balanced portfolio might include an Internet stock, an airline, a brewery, a car manufacturer, a department store, and a bank.

The easiest way to achieve portfolio diversification with a smaller investment is to use a mutual fund. Thousands of individual investors pool their resources, hire a fund manager, and share in the successes of the whole fund. This is a great way to invest your money without losing any sleep. Someone else is losing sleep over your money. There are entire books just on the subject of selecting mutual funds. Most of the popular money management magazines publish an annual issue on mutual funds, with top ratings of funds and some guidelines on choosing a fund. Try *Forbes, Money, Fortune,* and others. Back issues of these magazines are available at your local library.

A great many people try to time the market by attempting to guess when the market or an individual stock is going to peak or bottom out. A few investors have made huge gains, but you won't hear about the thousands of investors who quietly lost their shirts. In the words of the Wall Street adage, it's not timing the market; it's time in the market.

The ultimate expression of timing the market is day trading, where one starts the trading day with cash and ends with cash, by buying stocks during the day and selling them later in the same day. It is an unusual stock that gains as much as 20% of its value during an entire year, with many small jumps and dips over the year. If there are about 250 trading days in a year, this exceptional stock will, on average, appreciate by 1/12 of 1% each trading day. If you are trading 600 shares of a $30 stock ($18,000) and you are paying a commission of only $8 per trade, then if the exceptional stock does exactly what is expected of it and appreciates 1/12 of 1%, the trading costs will exactly wipe out the day's gains. You have to consistently and dramatically outguess the market just to make the same gain as picking a good mutual fund and letting it ride for a year.

My strong advice is to invest in stocks by way of a balanced, stable mutual fund and make sure it's safe enough that you'll not lose sleep over your investments, even if you don't check stock prices more than once a year.

But there is more to retirement planning than just investing a lot of money really well. You should also try to develop habits of living within your means and without debt. Avoiding credit card debt can give you a return of 18% on your money just by avoiding interest expense. Make plans to have your house completely paid for by the time you retire (perhaps using a 15-year mortgage) and it will take much less money from your retirement accounts to support you.

Chapter 23
How Much Will This Cost?

You should not plan to open your law practice unless you are prepared for the expenditures necessary to do so. Not only do you need to be prepared for the initial capital expenditure, but you also need to plan for the initial operating expenses. Although you should be able to rather quickly have the business paying its own operating expenses, much of the money you make in the first year should be spent reinvesting in the business and paying off your initial capital expenses. You should not count on the business as a source of income for your personal bills for a year.

Initial capital requirements

Fortunately, the most expensive part of opening a law practice is getting a law license. You already have that behind you, and the remaining expenditures are smaller than for most other businesses. Some of this list is no more than a checklist of things for you to think about, because they may or may not be applicable to your situation. For example, if you are officing at home and sharing another lawyer's conference room, you will need very little office furniture, and what you do need may be very inexpensive.

Likewise, even if you need some of the items on my checklist you may find that your cost for those items is significantly higher or lower than mine, depending on your taste and how willing you are to spend the time to shop around.

Many of the following are not truly capital expenditures in the financial accounting sense, but they are significant expenditures that you must make in the first month or so of opening your office, so I have listed them here.

First and last month's rent, security deposit $400 - $3,000

Desk, credenza, executive chair, conference table, side chairs/conference chairs $500 - $5,000

Bookshelves $50 - $500

Lateral filing cabinet $200 - $600

Supply cabinet $50 - $300

Copier with collator and feeder $1,000 - $3,000

Fax machine $100 - $300

Computer with monitor $2,000

Printer $350

Software $2,000

Law books and/or legal research service and/or CD-ROM service $500 - $5,000

Supplies (pens, paper, envelopes, paper clips, sticky notes, manila folders, hanging files, etc.) $700

Malpractice insurance policy $1,000 - $2,000

Monthly expenses

Continuing education (seminars and conferences) $100

Advertising (church newspaper, etc.) $100

Rent $500 - $2,000

Telephone bill including small yellow pages ad $100 - $500

Mobile telephone $100

Internet access and web hosting $20 - $50

Office supplies $100

Postage $100

Computer hardware and software $100

Online research, library updates, forms software $50 - $500

Allowance for income taxes: approximately ⅓ of income less tax-deductible expenses

Sources of financing

The most proven sources of financing for a law practice are borrowing on credit cards and borrowing from relatives (especially parents). The Small Business Administration also has start-up money for new businesses, but because of the paperwork involved, most banks will not entertain an SBA loan for less than about $80,000, which is far more than the average lawyer would need.

Some lawyers choose to work at some other job until they have saved up enough money to start the law practice. And many lawyers have lived off of their spouse's earnings until the law practice began producing.

Chapter 24
Final Thoughts

Starting your own law practice will not be easy, but nothing worthwhile ever is. But it isn't like a trip to the moon, where everything must be perfect or you'll perish. There are a large number of small steps, and the entire process can be taken in bite-sized pieces. You will make mistakes, but you will learn from them and do better next time. You will recover from every mistake. You will learn very quickly. You have advantages that Abraham Lincoln did not have with his career: you have two college degrees, very specialized training, wonderful office equipment, and professionally designed forms.

You do need a confidence boost. Join your local bar association and ask if there is a mentor program. Office with a helpful lawyer. Join a local young lawyers group. Take a lawyer to lunch. You'll find that most lawyers are friendly, helpful, and flattered that you asked. As big as your problems seem, every solo lawyer has been down the same road, and would like to spare you a mistake.

I wish you the best of luck, and hope you find the solo practice of law rewarding. Please send your success stories to hdavis@planolaw.com.